KRITZERLAND

Also by Bruce Kimmel

BENJAMIN KRITZER

KRITZERLAND

A novel by

Bruce Kimmel

ISBN: 1-4107-2885-4 (e-book)
ISBN: 1-4107-2884-6 (Paperback)
ISBN: 1-4107-2883-8 (Dust Jacket)

This book is printed on acid free paper.

Cover Painting by Harvey Schmidt

1stBooks – rev. 04/08/03

For Margaret

who believed I had another one in me

and who always kept me on the right road

And for my Aunt Bella, who was wonderful, warm, and

wise.

PROLOGUE

Benjamin Kritzer, Man

He was scared. More scared than he'd ever been in his entire life, and Benjamin Kritzer had been plenty scared before. After all, hadn't he been tormented by the Bad Men for years? Oh, yes, he'd been tormented by the Bad Men for years, but this was 1960 and he was thirteen now and the Bad Men seemed to have moved on, presumably to torment some other little boy. However, the Bad Men had been replaced by something equally as frightening to Benjamin Kritzer and, stranger still, the new, equally frightening thing had the same initials as the Bad Men. B.M. Only this time B.M. didn't stand for Bad Men. It stood for Bar Mitzvah.

Today was the day Benjamin Kritzer was going to be a man. That's what Rabbi Pressman had told him, that's what his Hebrew School teacher, Mrs. Slatinsky, had told him

1

and that's what his Martian parents, Ernie and Minnie Kritzer had told him. Yes, from today forward he would forever be known as Benjamin Kritzer, Man. Lately, he'd taken to answering the phone like that: "Benjamin Kritzer, Man," he'd say to whoever happened to be calling. He wanted to have business cards printed up like that—Benjamin Kritzer, Man—like Paladin had on *Have Gun, Will Travel.*

Benjamin Kritzer, Man, was sitting on the stage of Temple Beth Am (at least *he* thought of it as a stage), dressed in an ugly black suit, an ugly white shirt, an ugly tie, and ugly black shoes, and he looked about as comfortable as Janet Leigh after her shower in *Psycho.* He'd seen *Psycho* that summer at the El Rey Theater on Wilshire Boulevard and it had, as Minnie Kritzer put it, scared the bejeezus out of him. He didn't really know what the bejeezus was, but whatever it was, *Psycho* had scared it out of him, although apparently there was still some bejeezus left in him, given his current state.

Rabbi Pressman put his hand on Benjamin's knee, not so much in reassurance, but because Benjamin's knee was going up and down a mile a minute, like one of those oil pumps on La Cienega. His heart was thud-thudding in his chest, because soon he knew he'd be at the podium, soon he'd be going through his Bar Mitzvah ceremony, speaking all of the haftorah he'd so dutifully memorized. Soon he'd be making his "Today I am a man" speech, which he'd also dutifully memorized and rehearsed into the Webcor tape recorder that Ernie had dutifully bought him. He didn't know why he was so petrified—after all, it wasn't like he hadn't performed in front of people before. He'd been doing The Benjamin Kritzer Hour for years. But this was different, and although he'd survived the Bad Men, survived his brother Jeffrey (so far), survived being hit with the hanger, and even survived a broken heart, he was not at all certain he'd survive this.

Suddenly, Rabbi Pressman was standing up, which meant that Benjamin had to stand up. The Rabbi gestured for him to go to the podium. Benjamin rose from his chair in slow motion. He crossed to the podium in slow motion. Why was everything in slow motion, he wondered? He got to the podium and looked out at the congregation. Sitting in the second row were his parents and brother. Jeffrey was making faces at him, Ernie was sitting there, hands resting on his rotund belly with his eyes shut, and Minnie, wearing a lurid green dress (of course she was—what other color dress would a Martian wear?) and her pointy rhinestone glasses, was waving at him. Waving at him, for heaven's sake. That simply made Benjamin Kritzer want to vomit on the ground. Why did mothers behave that way? It was so embarrassing, but there she was, nevertheless, waving at him like some out-of-control train signal.

Benjamin took a deep breath, tried not to look at his family, and began reciting the haftorah.

"Barchu et adonai hamvorach..."

Out of the corner of his eye, Benjamin could see Jeffrey giving him the finger. Yes, today Benjamin was going to be a man, all right, and the first thing he would do as a man would be to stab Jeffrey with a kitchen knife when he got home. Benjamin's knee was still shaking uncontrollably and was actually hitting the podium, which added a nice rat-a-tat rhythm to his sing-songy recitation. He continued reciting as the congregation looked on, watching proudly as Benjamin Kritzer became a man.

Bruce Kimmel

PART ONE

New Adventures

"Well, you ask me if I'll forget my baby
I guess I will someday
I don't like it but I guess things happen that way
You ask me if I'll get along
I guess I will some way
I don't like it but I guess things happen that way"

—Johnny Cash, *Guess Things Happen That Way*,
Sun 45 295

Bruce Kimmel

CHAPTER ONE

The Return of Benjamin Kritzer

As it turned out, 1958 hadn't been such a bad year after all. Benjamin Kritzer had survived being ten, he'd entered the 6th grade and had a much better and nicer teacher than his 5th grade teacher, the old sourpuss, Miss Brady, and even his broken heart had started to mend. Oh, he still thought about Susan Pomeroy in far-off Canada, he still saw her as clear as daylight, still saw her beautiful face, still heard her mad giggle. He still looked through their Word Notebook at all their spelled-backwards words. In fact, he'd even begun adding to it—his latest had become one of his favorites: halb, halb, halb (it had come to him after Minnie Kritzer had said "blah, blah, blah" to him one fine day). Halb was a much better word than blah, and Benjamin ascribed a meaning to it—a halb was someone who sat in front of Benjamin at the movie theater.

Benjamin hated when people sat in front of him at the movie theater, and now he had a name for that person. If someone had the temerity to sit in front of Benjamin's tenth-row center-aisle seat, Benjamin would lean forward and quietly say "halb". If the person didn't move, then Benjamin would lean forward again and say "halb" louder. He would keep on saying it over and over—"halb, halb, halb"—until the person, not knowing why they were hearing this strange boy say "halb" over and over, would finally, mercifully, move to another seat. Benjamin called this The Halb Treatment, and it never failed to work.

Susan would have loved "halb" and The Halb Treatment, but Susan was in Canada and therefore had no knowledge of The Halb Treatment. Luckily, Benjamin still had the photos they'd taken at the photo booth at Ocean Park Pier the year before on Passover. Sometimes he'd take the photo strip out and take it into bed with him, and there he'd lie, covers over his head, with his transistor radio on his chest, earpiece in his ear, turning the dial until he found a song he loved (his current favorite was *Poor Little Fool* by Ricky Nelson), and a flashlight illuminating the photos of Susan and him.

* * *

Benjamin still felt he was unique, special, and he was still pretty much a loner. He still looked up girls' dresses at their lovely cotton underpants, he still stopped at Marty's Bike and Candy Shop for his daily dose of red licorice, and he was still amassing quite a collection of 45s, which he played incessantly on his 45rpm record player, one after another.

Benjamin had finally begun to be himself again that previous May. There were several reasons for this. One of them was that he didn't want to hear his mother say, "Benjamin, you are not yourself" anymore. Every day she would say it—"Benjamin, you are not yourself"—until he wanted to scream, "Who am I then, Perry Como?"

One night, he was lying in bed, covers over his head, flipping around the dial of his transistor radio, when he heard a new song by someone named Johnny Cash and the Tennessee Two. It instantly became his favorite, and he ran to Index Records and Radio the next day and bought the 45. It was on the Sun label. When he got home he put the record on his 45rpm record player and let it repeat over and over and over again.

You ask me if I'll forget my baby
I guess I will some day
I don't like it but I guess things happen that way

Wasn't that just what he was feeling in a nutshell? Didn't that just hit the nail on the head?

You ask me if I'll get along
I guess I will some way
I don't like it but I guess things happen that way

For weeks he walked around singing that song. Whenever Minnie would ask him anything, any question at all, such as, "Is it necessary for your room to look like a tornado hit it?" he'd look at her for a moment, and then sing, "I don't like it but I guess things happen that way." Of course, after a few days of this, Minnie Kritzer began to

9

get migraines, and she would say, "Shut up with that song already, Benjamin, do you enjoy giving your mother a headache?" to which Benjamin, of course, would reply, "I don't like it but I guess things happen that way," followed by "Ba doo ba doo, ba doo ba doo", which would send Minnie straight into her bedroom, muttering, "Ba doo ba doo. What kind of music is that?" She'd then lie down on her bed with her usual Witch Hazel pads on her eyes, while Benjamin went about his business, singing, "I don't like it but I guess things happen that way."

* * *

Another thing that helped Benjamin become himself happened in June of 1958, with the opening of Pacific Ocean Park.

He'd watched it being built, peeked through the wooden boards surrounding it, looked out the window of his grandparents' apartment at the Hotel St. Regis (which afforded quite a nice view), and he couldn't wait until opening day arrived.

As that day approached, he began to pester his mother about wanting to be first in line, how it was imperative that he be first in line. Minnie Kritzer didn't seem to care one way or another if Benjamin was first in line and she told him so, and when he kept on about it, she looked at him and sang, "I don't like it but I guess things happen that way" followed by "Ba doo ba doo, ba doo ba doo". That annoyed Benjamin most of all—how dare she use his very own annoying thing to annoy him in return? Where was the fairness in *that*? But he kept on and on about wanting to be first in line. After about the hundredth time he brought it up, Minnie turned to him with a fatigued look on her face and said, "Benjamin, we will do the best we can. We will try to get there early enough so you can be first in line. Can you shut up now?"

"I can, as long as I'm first in line," Benjamin replied.

Minnie rolled her eyes heavenward and exhaled loudly. "Benjamin, you really take the cake."

Benjamin looked at his mother. "I take the cake?"

Minnie looked right back at Benjamin. "You know what I mean."

"I took the cake? I didn't even know there *was* a cake."

"Shut up, Benjamin. It's a saying, you know it's a saying."

"Fine, it's a saying. What does it *mean?*"

"It means you take the cake."

"What cake, what cake? Show me some cake and I'll take it, then the saying will at least make sense."

"Benjamin, go play in traffic."

"I should play in traffic because I took the cake?"

"You keep this up and you will definitely not be first in line. You know, you can't have your cake and eat it, too."

Benjamin's face began to resemble a waffle. "I can't have my cake and eat it, too? If I take the cake I just have to look at it? Why can't I have my cake and eat it too?"

"Because sometimes life doesn't work out the way we want it to," Minnie said with an edge creeping into her voice. Benjamin didn't like an edge creeping into her voice so he dropped the subject of taking the cake and eating or not eating it.

* * *

He was first in line. The Kritzers had arisen and were out of the house by eight o'clock that morning. The sun was already out and the sky was that Los Angeles kind of blue you only saw in Technicolor movies (rather than movies with Color by DeLuxe—Benjamin did not like Color by DeLuxe, he didn't think it sparkled like Technicolor). They'd arrived at the beach by eight-thirty and gone directly to the Hotel St. Regis to see Grandma and Grandpa Gelfinbaum. Grandpa Gelfinbaum was in an especially foul mood and he refused to go down and see the new amusement park; he was still very bitter that his Wheel O' Fortune stand had been shuttered, along with the rest of Ocean Park Pier. When Minnie Kritzer suggested to him that he come down with the rest of them, he'd taken the slimy wet cigar out of his mouth, hocked a glob of brown spit in the kitchen sink and said, "What is it, fish?"

Ernie gave Benjamin and Jeffrey each five dollars and they ran down the three flights of stairs (faster than taking the old rickety St. Regis elevator), ran across the boardwalk to the entrance which, as it so happened, was conveniently located directly across from the St. Regis.

From his place in the front of the line, right by the entrance to Neptune's Kingdom, Benjamin could see that the dome of the Dome movie theater was still there, and, even though there was a new façade around where the actual theater had been, he wondered if it was still there, hidden behind the colorful wooden walls. He could also see the International Promenade, with its brightly-painted stores and restaurants, which now lined the boardwalk. He thought it strange that he would now have to pay to enter a place that he used to enter for free, but that was progress for you.

As ten o'clock approached, the line had gotten quite long, and in fact Benjamin couldn't even see the end of it. Apparently, the lure of this new Disneyland-by-the-ocean had been irresistible, because there were hundreds upon hundreds of people waiting for their first glimpse of Pacific Ocean Park. Adults, teenagers, noisy children, all dressed in colorful summer attire, all waiting, like Benjamin, for the gates to open.

At ten sharp, POP officially opened, and Benjamin bought his ticket and walked through the gate, followed by Jeffrey. They went into Neptune's Kingdom. It was like *20,000 Leagues Under the Sea,* Neptune's Kingdom was, with giant glassed-in tanks with thousands of exotic fish swimming about, merrily showing off to their first audience. Benjamin turned to Jeffrey and said, "What is it, fish?" to which Jeffrey replied, "I hope it gets better than this. This is boring." They moved quickly through the Kingdom and came out through a large opening and were suddenly on the main grounds of the park.

As he looked around, Benjamin was amazed that a place he'd been to hundreds of times could look so different. In fact, the only thing that he saw that looked remotely the same was the roller coaster, and even that had been gussied up and given a brand spanking new paint job. Yet somehow all that new paint could not quite disguise the inherent seediness of what had once been Ocean Park Pier.

Jeffrey went off on his own, not wanting to be burdened with Benjamin and that, of course, was fine with Benjamin, who didn't want to be burdened with Jeffrey. Benjamin couldn't decide which way to go first. He saw the Sea Circus straight ahead of him, but that wasn't of much interest. He looked up and saw what appeared to be big plastic bubbles which were on big cables that traveled across the length of the park—the Ocean Skyway. He'd go on that in a little while, even though heights made him nauseous. He turned, and off in the distance, he saw a big building with a colorful front near where the Dome Theater had been—the Magic Carpet Ride. Well, that sounded right up Benjamin Kritzer's alley so he headed in that direction. As he walked, he happened to glance to his left and saw a ride which made him stop in his tracks. He walked over to it and stared at the sign, not believing that such a ride could exist. Flight to Mars, the sign read. That was just too irresistible, the Flight to Mars, and he suddenly forgot all about the Magic Carpet Ride, because finally Benjamin Kritzer would get to visit the planet his parents had come from.

He got in line (it was thankfully not long), and after a short wait entered the building that housed the ride. The first thing that happened was that everyone got on a conveyor belt, which carried them towards the door to the spaceship, while a soothing voice told them all about the planet Mars.

As they were carried past a white wall, flashes went off, like a camera taking a flash photo. Suddenly everyone's shadow (Benjamin's included) was seemingly imprinted on the white wall. Benjamin was so enthralled with seeing his very own shadow imprinted on the white wall that he missed what the soothing voice was saying, so he had no idea *why* all these shadows had been imprinted on the white wall. He supposed it had something to do with Mars—after all, the ride was called Flight to Mars, wasn't it?

As they continued on the conveyor belt, the soothing voice told them they'd be entering a spaceship and would be taking a flight to Mars. Finally, they entered the spaceship. Benjamin immediately found the best seat and strapped himself in. Everyone else found their seats and did the same.

A large telescreen came alive and an image of Pacific Ocean Park came up. A voice instructed everyone to make certain they were strapped in securely for their trip to Mars. The voice then began a countdown—"10, 9, 8, 7..." Suddenly there was a tremendously loud noise—"6, 5, 4..." The noise got louder and louder—"3, 2, 1...Blast off!" The loud noise got even louder as the whole spaceship began to shake and vibrate. On the telescreen, Benjamin could see that they were becoming airborne, that Pacific Ocean Park was being left behind, replaced by sky and clouds and finally blackness and stars. Oh, this was exciting, this Flight to Mars was. The voice droned on, but Benjamin couldn't pay attention because he was going to Mars.

The rest of the trip happened rather quickly—on the telescreen they could see the landing on Mars, see the Marsscape and the voice gave several pertinent facts. But the voice said nothing about the Kritzers. How could the voice ignore Ernie and Minnie Kritzer, two of Mars' finest denizens? A few minutes later, Benjamin was back on Earth, specifically back at Pacific Ocean Park. He came out the exit door into blinding sunlight and actually had to stop for a minute to regain his vision.

* * *

By one o'clock he'd already been to Mars four times. Benjamin simply could not get enough of Mars. He'd also gone on the Ocean Skyway, which was quite frightening for him and yet afforded a beautiful view of the entire new amusement park: He'd been on the Magic Carpet Ride, which he didn't find all that magical, and he'd walked everywhere and covered every inch of Pacific Ocean Park.

Certain rides he wouldn't go near—the roller coaster and the Ferris wheel being two of them. There was no way Benjamin Kritzer would ever go on that roller coaster because Jeffrey Kritzer had told him a story that cousin Denny had recounted—how one fine day some idiot had stood up and been decapitated. Benjamin simply would not go on any ride where there was danger of decapitation. As to the Ferris wheel, he had a tremendous fear that it would get stuck and leave him stranded at the very top. Being stranded at the top of a Ferris wheel was not acceptable to Benjamin Kritzer. But he did visit the South Sea Island (boring), and the Enchanted Forest with its Dream House, Atomic City and reproduction of the Nautilus nuclear-powered submarine. He enjoyed the Enchanted Forest because he liked anything that was futuristic and weird. He also went on the Diving Bells and, while it was no Flight to Mars, it was mildly amusing.

Mostly he marveled at the fact that he couldn't remember where things had been—couldn't even figure out where Grandpa Gelfinbaum's Wheel O' Fortune had been. Only a year had passed and it was almost like those things had never existed. No Toonerville, no pitching dimes to win a two-dollar bill, no Vanilla Custard Ice Cream stand. However, the House of Mirrors was still where it used to be and so was the Arcade, although many of Benjamin's favorite games had been removed and replaced with newer and less-interesting ones.

There were many new food stands and souvenir shops, and everyone seemed to be having a fine time discovering all the attractions. At two-thirty he finally exited the park, the exit being quite near where the Dome Theater had been. He walked along the boardwalk, back towards the St. Regis, looking at all the new shops and restaurants. The shop he was most intrigued by wasn't open yet—there was a sign in the window that said "Open Soon"—it was a magic shop and just looking at some of the things in the window made Benjamin want to go into that shop very much.

He took the scary elevator up to the third floor, got off and walked down the musty hallway towards his grandparents' apartment. He opened the door and was immediately greeted by the smell of canned salmon and onions. Jeffrey was already there, watching *American Bandstand* on the Gelfinbaums' tiny television. Ernie was sitting in a chair, asleep and snoring loudly. Minnie was in the kitchen washing dishes with Grandma Gelfinbaum. Grandpa Gelfinbaum was nowhere to be seen, although a moment later Benjamin heard grunting and groaning coming from the bathroom and he knew that Grandpa Gelfinbaum was having a stool episode. Some things would never change, Benjamin thought.

All in all, his first visit to Pacific Ocean Park had been fun. He'd go back and go back often—and were they to give an award for most trips to Mars, he was quite certain that he'd be the winner.

* * *

It seemed that every song Benjamin heard on the radio that year somehow captured his feelings—first *Guess Things*

Happen That Way, and then *It's All in the Game*, which he heard one fine night on his Sony TR63 transistor radio. Tommy Edwards' beautiful voice wafted through Benjamin's earpiece.

> *Many a tear has to fall*
> *But it's all in the game*
> *All in the wonderful game*
> *That we know as love*

Wasn't that the truth? Many a tear *had* fallen and it was all in the game so he bought that 45, too, and he added it to the growing stack of records that he played over and over again. As if those two songs weren't enough, then came the Everly Brothers' *All I Have To Do Is Dream*—and again a song magically captured what Benjamin felt.

> *When I want you in my arms*
> *When I need you and all your charms*
> *Whenever I want you all I have to do is dream*

It was as if all those songs had been written expressly for him, and when he played them they brought back Susan to him so vividly it was almost as if she were there. She wasn't there, of course, but it was the next best thing, Benjamin supposed.

Of course, not every song Benjamin heard and loved reminded him of Susan. Certainly *The Purple People Eater* didn't remind him of Susan. Neither did *The Chipmunk Song*, *The Blob* or *Witch Doctor*. As it so happened, 1958 turned out to be a great year for songs, and it seemed that every time Benjamin turned on the radio he fell in love with a new one—*Volare, Secretly, Twilight Time, 26 Miles, Splish Splash,* and on and on.

* * *

Benjamin was petrified of animals. The reason for this was simple: Minnie Kritzer was petrified of animals. Animals terrified her, and she instilled this fear into both her children, although it didn't bother Jeffrey that much. On the other hand, it most assuredly bothered Benjamin.

An example of what she drummed into Benjamin from an early age would be the following: That cats, those seemingly adorable little critters, those furry soft purring pets, sucked baby's breath and were horrifying terrible creatures that should not be trusted because, adorable furry soft purring little critters though they might appear, not only did they suck baby's breath (Benjamin didn't understand what that meant but whatever it meant it couldn't be good), they also clawed you and left ugly scratch marks all over your arms. Then there were dogs. She told him that while she was sure that some dogs were nice, others were frothing rabid beasts that would bite people and rip the flesh from their very bodies.

Needless to say, there were no animals in the Kritzer household. Benjamin was told to stay away from them in the street. Even sweet-looking birds were suspect and could, according to Minnie, peck your eyes out at any minute. And heaven forbid if a fly had the audacity to intrude into the Kritzer house. Out would come the fly-swatter and Minnie would methodically hunt down the offending fly, no matter how long it took, until she'd cornered it and swatted the very life out of it.

Then there was the little matter of bees. As a child, Minnie had been stung by a bee, and she'd never gotten over it. The incident had grown in her mind to epic proportions and she warned Benjamin about bees and their lethal stingers and how you could die from being stung or, at the very least, puff up like a balloon until you were unrecognizable as a human being. All of those stories had indeed made Benjamin terrified of cats, dogs, birds and yes, most especially bees. Then, in July of 1958, Benjamin had come face to face with this instilled terror, twice in one week.

The first episode happened on a Wednesday. Benjamin was on his way to the first show at the Lido Theater to see Alfred Hitchcock's *Vertigo*. He was walking down Sherbourne Drive, dressed in his brand spanking new calypso pants (with a navy-blue stripe down each side), calypso shirt tied at the waist, and on his feet were a nice pair of thongs. He looked like a short Jewish ten-year-old Harry Belafonte. About a block before he reached Pico, a dog suddenly appeared out of nowhere, barking wildly, scaring Benjamin half out of his wits. Benjamin just stood there, not sure what to do. The dog seemed really angry (maybe it didn't like the calypso pants, Benjamin thought) and was baring its quite pointy teeth at Benjamin in a really vicious way. Benjamin looked around, but it was just him and the dog, there was no one else in sight. The dog was now growling, a low sickening growl. Then it started barking again. Benjamin thought about his options. He could try reasoning with the dog, try being friendly to the dog—maybe if he sang *Volare* the dog would calm down. Benjamin looked at the dog, and quietly started singing.

"Volare, oh, oh Cantare, oh, oh, oh, oh"

The dog stopped barking for a moment and just looked at Benjamin quizzically. It was working, Benjamin thought, and he continued singing.

"Nel blu dipinto di blu"

The dog went crazy, snapping, barking, growling and actually drooling. Benjamin crazily thought that maybe the dog didn't like Italian. Totally panicked now, Benjamin quickly decided that he had two choices: He could stand there and miss the beginning of *Vertigo* or he could make a run for it. The former was not an option (Benjamin would rather die than miss the beginning of a movie), and so he chose the latter. He took a deep breath, then suddenly looked behind the dog and waved and said, "Hi." The dog turned to see who Benjamin was saying "Hi" to (there was no one there—it had been a clever ploy on Benjamin's part), and Benjamin began to run like the wind. The dog turned around and lunged at Benjamin and managed to clamp its teeth on Benjamin's left thong, which came loose. Benjamin kept on going, one bare foot and one thong, the thong thwacking against the pavement. He didn't look back, but since the dog's barking was receding into the distance he presumed the dog was busy ripping his left thong to shreds (better the thong than him, Benjamin thought). His adrenaline was on high, and he tried to calm down as he walked unevenly the rest of the way to the Lido. Luckily, no one seemed to notice that one foot was bare and one had a thong.

Vertigo made him forget all about the terrifying encounter with the dog. He was mesmerized by the movie, even though he didn't really understand what was going on.

The second episode happened the following Monday. Benjamin was in the back yard, playing by himself. He was

21

in one of his imaginary adventures, when he happened to look up toward one of the tall honeysuckle bushes that lined the yard. There, much to his horror, he spied a huge bee. This was not merely a bee, no, this was a *BEE*; this was the largest *BEE* ever put on earth, this was a big black ugly *BEE* the size of a plate. It was buzzing loudly around the honeysuckle bush. Benjamin looked at that big huge enormous ugly black bee and his mother's words rang in his ears loudly—if you see a bee, don't move! Any sudden movement and that bee would immediately come over to you, look you squarely in the eye and then sting the living daylights out of you. Benjamin didn't really know what the living daylights were, but he most certainly did not want them stung out of him.

He stood there, frozen, not moving an inch. He stared at the bee, which continued to buzz around the honeysuckle bush. Benjamin thought about moving, thought about running, but his fear was too great to do anything but stand there as still as a statue until the bee flew away.

The sun was beating down, and unfortunately Benjamin was facing it. Beads of sweat broke out on his forehead and began to trickle down his face. He was too scared to even wipe the dripping sweat away. He was quite certain that if he so much as lifted his arm to wipe the sweat away, the bee would swing around, zoom towards him, look him squarely in the eye, and sting the living daylights out of him. And so he stood there and stood there and sweated and sweated, while the bee, oblivious to the young sweating boy, buzzed around the honeysuckle bush quite contentedly, as if it had nothing else to do in the whole world.

Three hours later, Benjamin was still standing there, and the bee was still buzzing around the honeysuckle bush, which Benjamin now hated with a vengeance. Oh, how he hated that honeysuckle bush, he wanted to rip the living daylights out of that honeysuckle bush, and he would have, except he couldn't move because the bee was still buzzing and if he moved it most certainly would come and sting him and he would die or puff up like a balloon. He was drenched in sweat by this time, and his face had begun to turn a nice bright shade of red from the relentless sun. Finally, mercifully, the bee dived, zoomed, and then suddenly decided it had had enough of the Kritzers' backyard, and off it went on its merry way.

The minute the coast was clear, Benjamin ran from the yard and back into the house. Minnie was still out having her hair done, and Jeffrey was in the kitchen drinking milk out of the carton (Benjamin found that nauseating) and eating from a package of Fig Newtons. Jeffrey looked at his dripping-with-sweat brother.

"What's the matter with you?"

"Bee. There was a bee. I could have been killed."

Jeffrey shoved the package of Fig Newtons toward Benjamin. "Here, eat a Fig Newton, you'll feel better."

"Eat a Fig Newton? This is what you say to someone who could have been killed by a bee?"

"You want an Oreo instead?"

There was no reasoning with a Fig Newton-munching brother, so Benjamin went to his room, went into the closet and removed his drenched clothing, put on some shorts and a shirt, and watched television for the rest of the day. He didn't go in the backyard for an entire week.

* * *

23

Those weren't the only exciting events of 1958, not by a long shot. Benjamin had seen many wonderful movies during the year, including his favorite, *The Seventh Voyage of Sinbad*. Oh, how he loved *The Seventh Voyage of Sinbad*; that was just the finest motion picture ever made, in Benjamin Kritzer's humble opinion. It had everything—it had Sinbad, it had a shrunken princess, it had an evil magician (Benjamin loved when the evil magician said, "Kill him. Kill him"—the way the magician pronounced it sounded like "Kill hin, kill hin"), it had a one-eyed Cyclops, a bird with two heads, and a dragon, not to mention a genie in a bottle. Benjamin saw *The Seventh Voyage of Sinbad* four times during its run at the Stadium Theater. He would go home and pretend he was Sinbad, unless Jeffrey was annoying him, in which case he'd pretend he was the evil magician— Benjamin would cast an evil eye at Jeffrey and say, in his scariest voice, "Kill hin, kill hin."

Another exciting thing that happened that year happened in August, down the street from Benjamin, at the Betlemans' house. The Betlemans' maid had gotten in her car and meant to back out of the driveway. Unfortunately, she'd put the car in drive instead of reverse, and she'd driven right through the front of the Betlemans' house. Everyone on the block had gone running to see what had happened, and Benjamin was no exception. It was quite a sight, the maid's 1951 Nash Rambler protruding into the Betlemans' dining room. The maid was quite distraught at having driven into the front of the Betlemans' house, which she'd apparently just finished cleaning. The Betlemans calmed her down and told her there was no problem and that everything would be fine. And that was true, except for the fact that the Betlemans soon thereafter fired her.

Benjamin had told Lulu Salmon, the Kritzers' cleaning lady, about the incident, and she'd bellowed loudly, "Well, that's why I take the bus!"

*   *   *

However, the *most* exciting thing that happened in 1958 was the day Benjamin got to visit Paramount Studios. How it happened was this: One of Minnie's friends knew someone at the studio and, knowing Benjamin's love of movies, she invited Minnie and Benjamin to come watch a movie being shot. Minnie told Benjamin about it and Benjamin was ecstatic. He was beyond ecstatic. He was in heaven—just the thought of visiting Paramount Studios (his favorite—after all they had VistaVision) sent him into paroxysms of excitement. So much so that Minnie finally had to laugh.

"Benjamin, I've never seen you this excited," she said. "You're beside yourself."

Benjamin, who was in the middle of drinking the red-colored liquid from a wax stick, stopped mid-drink and looked at his mother. "I'm beside myself?"

Minnie shook her head. "You know what I mean, Benjamin. You are beside yourself with excitement."

Benjamin looked to his right and to his left, then back to his mother. "I'm not beside myself, how can I be beside myself?"

"Do you want to go to Paramount Studios, Benjamin?"

"Yes, yes, yes!"

"Then you are beside yourself and that is the end of this conversation."

"You're right, I'm beside myself," Benjamin said quickly. "And look who's standing next to us—excitement."

"What?"

"You said I was beside myself with excitement. So, that means there's me, myself and excitement."

"Benjamin, must you be such a weird child? Why do you have to take everything to the nth degree?"

Benjamin didn't know he always took everything to the nth degree; that was news to him. Nor did he even know what the nth degree was, but he figured now was not a good time to ask because, after all, he was going to Paramount Studios. He finished drinking the liquid from the wax stick and then put his brand new pair of wax lips in his mouth (he was currently very enamored of wax sticks and wax lips) and quickly went to his room.

A week later Benjamin was dressed in a pair of his nicest pants, with a nice shirt, his nice shoes, (his hair was combed quite nicely as well) and he and his mother were on their way to Paramount Studios. The whole way, up La Cienega, east on Melrose, Benjamin's leg was going up and down a mile a minute.

His leg had always done that, as long as he could remember, whenever he was antsy or excited. Jeffrey had told him that it was because Mae, the cleaning lady they'd had when Benjamin was a baby, used to tie Benjamin's feet together when he was in the crib, because apparently he would kick ferociously. Benjamin didn't know if Jeffrey was making that up or not, but it made perfect sense to him.

In any case, his leg was going up and down a mile a minute and was getting worse the more they drove. Minnie looked over at Benjamin's leg and said, "Benjamin, stop with the leg already, will you?" Benjamin tried to stop with the leg already, did his best to stop with the leg already, but it was a losing battle. His leg just had a will of its own and that was all there was to it.

Minnie turned left onto a small street, and suddenly there, looming before them, were the huge Paramount gates. Minnie drove forward and told the guard who she was and who they were meeting. The guard went into a booth, looked at a piece of paper, then came back out and told Minnie where to park the car.

After parking, she and Benjamin came back to the gate and were given directions to the sound stage they were going to. As they walked across the lot, Benjamin saw people in costumes wandering about, as if they had somehow gotten lost in a world they didn't belong to. There were cowboys, Indians, gangsters, beautiful showgirls (one of them waved at Benjamin as he stared at her, wide-eyed)—every kind of character Benjamin had seen in the movies was there. Finally, they reached the stage where Minnie's friend (the one who knew someone) was waiting. Minnie and her friend, Helen, hugged and then Helen gave Benjamin a hug, which he didn't mind at all because Helen was quite pretty. Helen told them that once they entered the stage they had to be very quiet and just watch. With that, Helen opened the stage door and the three of them went in.

Benjamin could not believe his eyes—he'd never seen such activity in his life. There were people everywhere, hustling and bustling, some moving equipment, some moving huge lights, while others just stood around—but even the people who were just standing around appeared animated and energized, and it seemed like everyone was talking at once. Helen led them toward the set where the scene was being shot. As they walked, they passed by a cartoony-looking set, although it wasn't lit and was empty. Off in a corner was another set, this one brightly lit, almost blindingly so. Helen brought them forward until they had a clear view of the set. To his right, Benjamin could see the huge VistaVision camera (it had the logo on the side—he loved that logo). On the set were a few actors, who were getting ready to do a scene. Helen leaned over and whispered to Minnie and Benjamin.

"The movie they're making is called *Li'l Abner.* Right now, they're shooting a scene with General Bullmoose."

Minnie nodded as if she knew what that meant. Benjamin, of course, had no idea who or what a General Bullmoose was and he really didn't care because he could not take his eyes off the huge VistaVision camera. He decided he wanted one of his very own. Suddenly someone was shouting, "Quiet—we're ready for a take," and all of a sudden all the activity and noise stopped, just like that. Another voice said, "Rolling," then "Speed," then another voice said, "Action."

One of the actors was bellowing loudly (presumably General Bullmoose), while next to him, lying across a large desk with dollar signs on it, was a very pretty lady wearing a low-cut dress and a huge fur, who kept saying, "But *Bullsie.*" She said it several times in response to the bellowing General Bullmoose. After the third time, a voice yelled, "Cut. Let's go again, right away." The actors got back into the positions they'd been in at the beginning, then the same voices as before said, "Rolling," then "Speed," then "Action." Then the actors did exactly the same thing again. Again, a voice said, "Cut." And again they did the scene.

After the fourth time, Benjamin turned to Minnie and Helen.

"Why do they keep doing the same thing over and over again?" he whispered.

Helen whispered back, "Because the director must not be happy with what they're doing."

This was all so confusing. The first time they'd done it had seemed perfectly fine to Benjamin (he'd laughed silently because he'd been instructed not to make any noise), and each successive time they'd done it had seemed perfectly fine to Benjamin. And yet, on they went, doing it again and again, because someone called "the director" wasn't happy. He imagined it must have been very boring for the pretty lady to keep saying, "But *Bullsie*" over and over again. Finally, after the seventh time, a voice said "Cut," followed by "Print." Suddenly, everyone was hustling and bustling again and the big VistaVision camera was being moved to a different part of the set. Benjamin wondered if this was the way every movie was made. If they did that scene seven times, was it going to be in the movie seven times? That would be very annoying, Benjamin thought.

They stood there for another hour, and then they watched the next scene, which was actually the same scene over again with the camera filming a different actor. That took an hour, and then it was time for them to leave. As Helen walked them back to the door, Benjamin saw a sight that made his jaw drop—an incredibly beautiful blonde woman wearing the smallest dress he'd ever seen in his young life. He just stopped in his tracks and stared at her. Minnie tugged on his arm but he couldn't or wouldn't budge. Helen saw Benjamin staring and started to laugh. She leaned over to Benjamin and said, "Do you want to meet her?" Benjamin smiled a rather goony smile and nodded his head "yes". Helen took Benjamin by the hand and they all walked over to the blonde woman in the small dress.

"Benjamin Kritzer meet Daisy Mae," Helen said. Benjamin just stood there, unable to alter his idiotic grin.

Daisy Mae—wasn't that the most beautiful name in the whole world? Daisy Mae smiled at Benjamin and his heart started dancing like one of those couples on *American Bandstand*.

"Hello, Benjamin, welcome to Dogpatch. Are you having fun?"

Benjamin stood there with his grin plastered on his face like something that had been glued over his real mouth. Minnie nudged him, which brought him out of his trance.

"Hi. We had a cleaning lady named Mae once—she used to tie my feet together."

Well, that was a conversation ender, wasn't it? What on earth was he thinking of? Why had that just popped out like an unwanted watermelon seed? Daisy Mae was laughing.

"Well, my name is really Leslie Parrish. I play Daisy Mae in the movie. And I promise I won't tie your feet together."

Benjamin thought that having his feet tied together by Daisy Mae/Leslie Parrish would not be such a bad thing. Oh, no, she could come over to his house and tie his feet together anytime she liked. Daisy Mae/Leslie Parrish was smiling at Benjamin. "It was very nice to meet you, Benjamin. Go see the movie when it comes out." She leaned over and gave him a kiss on the cheek, and the smell of her was so sweet that it actually made him dizzy. Then she walked over to where the camera was.

All the way home Benjamin thought about Daisy Mae/Leslie Parrish and the way she'd kissed him on the cheek, and he knew that he'd be first in line whenever *Li'l Abner* came out.

* * *

For the rest of the year and for some time thereafter, Benjamin would imagine himself being filmed by the huge VistaVision camera. He would awaken in the morning and he'd pretend the camera was filming him getting out of bed. He'd get out of bed, then he'd get back in again and then get out again, just in case "the director" wasn't happy. Sometimes he'd get in and out of bed five or six times, just to make sure he'd done it the best he could. He'd walk down the street and imagine the huge VistaVision camera filming him. He'd eat dinner and imagine the huge VistaVision camera filming him. Someday, he imagined, he'd go to one of his favorite movie theaters and see his life on the big screen—Paramount Pictures Presents Benjamin Kritzer, starring Benjamin Kritzer, in Technicolor and, most importantly, VistaVision.

* * *

Yes, 1958 hadn't been such a bad year after all. Benjamin was pretty much back to being his old self. In December he turned eleven. And whenever he'd miss Susan or anything would happen that he didn't like, he'd simply sing, "I don't like it but I guess things happen that way. Ba doo ba doo, ba doo ba doo," and that made him feel just fine and dandy. Benjamin Kritzer was now eleven years old and ready to take on whatever life had in store for him. Or so he thought.

CHAPTER TWO

The Amazing Benjamin, and Kritzerland

Benjamin's favorite place at Pacific Ocean Park (other than the Flight to Mars ride) had become the magic shop on the boardwalk promenade, the House of Magic. Benjamin would spend hours in the shop, looking at the display cases full of tricks. On a shelf behind the counter were the larger tricks, plus a wonderful assortment of masks and hats and wands and ventriloquist dummies. In fact, Benjamin had gotten a Jerry Mahoney dummy from the House of Magic for Christmas.

The owner, Mr. Szymond, liked Benjamin and was always showing him the latest tricks. He was quite a good magician, Mr. Szymond was, and Benjamin was amazed and astounded at every card trick or disappearing ball or magical connecting-and-disconnecting rings that he would be shown. Benjamin had even purchased a few of the less expensive tricks and began practicing them for hours on end in preparation for one of his Monday night The Benjamin Kritzer Hours.

His favorite magic trick was the astounding guillotine trick. First, the magician, in this case The Amazing Benjamin (as he'd named himself), would insert an ordinary cigarette into a small hole at the bottom of the guillotine. He would then raise the sharp metal blade and then with sudden swiftness he'd lower the sharp metal blade, cutting the ordinary cigarette in half. So far, so good. He would then place a brand new ordinary cigarette in the small hole. He would then raise the sharp metal blade once again. And then, he would ask a volunteer (Benjamin was his own volunteer because no one else in the house wanted to go anywhere near that guillotine) to insert their finger into the bigger hole above the cigarette. Once said finger was inserted, The Amazing Benjamin would swiftly lower the sharp metal blade, which would magically pass through the inserted finger leaving it safe and sound, but still cutting the ordinary cigarette beneath it neatly in two.

It never occurred to Benjamin that had he armed the machine wrong (it had a rotating set of blades—one that went straight down, and one that went around the finger) that he actually might have cut off someone's finger, or at least given someone's finger a nice deep gash. No, that never occurred to Benjamin because he was The Amazing Benjamin and such a thing could never happen with The Amazing Benjamin doing the trick.

Finally, Benjamin was ready to unveil his new magic and ventriloquist act during The Benjamin Kritzer Hour (he'd already tried out the entire show on Leo, at Leo's

Delicatessen, and Leo had rewarded him with a free Dad's Root Beer, high praise indeed). The family assembled as they always did, directly after dinner (brisket and potatoes) on Monday night. First, The Amazing Benjamin did a routine with his Jerry Mahoney dummy. He'd written a script and everything and learned it by heart, and he performed it with great élan (it was modeled after his favorite Abbott and Costello routine, *Who's on First*). He called it Fine and Dandy. Benjamin played Dandy (sitting on Benjamin's head was a rubber fried egg he'd bought at the magic store), and the Jerry Mahoney dummy was Fine—the voice he used for the "dummy" sounded suspiciously like Grandpa Gelfinbaum.

Benjamin looked at the dummy and said, "Hello, you're looking fine today."

Then, in his Grandpa Gelfinbaum voice, the dummy replied, "Of course I look Fine. I *am* Fine. When you're Fine you look Fine."

"I'm fine, too, thanks for asking."

"You're Fine, too? That's a coincidence. Are we related?"

"Where do you come up with these things, you dummy? I say I'm fine, and you say 'are we related'."

"Well, if you're Fine and I'm Fine we might be related. And why do you have a fried egg on your head?"

"I'll get to that later. Listen, dummy, why, if we're both fine does that make us related? Your logic defies me."

"Well, my logic doesn't like you. All right, we're not related. How could I be related to someone like you? There, are you happy? Do you feel dandy now?"

Benjamin looked out at his audience and they were all chuckling. Grandma Gelfinbaum leaned over and punched

Grandpa Gelfinbaum on the arm and whispered, "The dummy sounds like you."

Benjamin continued. "How else should I feel? I'm Dandy, of course I feel Dandy."

"Good. I'm dandy, too."

"You're Dandy, too? Are we related?"

"How are we related, you schlemiel? I'm *Fine*."

"You just said you were Dandy."

"I'm Fine and I'm dandy. And why do you have that fried egg on your head?"

"I'll get to that later. Listen, you can be fine, but you can't be Dandy because *I'm* Dandy."

"Okay, already, I'm not dandy."

"Fine."

"What?"

"Fine."

"What?"

"What do you mean 'what'?"

"You said 'Fine'. I said 'what'."

"Why would you say 'what'? Didn't you hear me?"

"I heard you, I heard you, how can you not hear you, you never shut up. You said 'Fine'. When people say 'Fine' I say 'what'. And why do you have that fried egg on your head?"

"I'll get to that later. Well, remind me not to say hello to you next time I see you."

"Dandy."

"What?"

"Dandy."

"What?"

"Are you deaf?"

"No, I'm Dandy."

"I'm dandy, too. We're both dandy."

"That would be a fine kettle of fish."

"The Fine kettle of fish is at my house, which is a Fine house if I do say so myself."

"I don't even know what you're talking about anymore. I've got to go. It was nice seeing you again and I hope it's the last time. Wouldn't that be fine?"

"That would be dandy. And why do you have that fried egg on your head?"

"Well, if you must know, I had a different egg on my head but somebody poached it."

"Oh, that's just dandy."

"That's just fine."

Benjamin and the dummy looked at each other, then at the audience, and bowed. Everyone applauded, except Ernie, who'd fallen asleep and was snoring loudly. Minnie elbowed him in the ribs and he woke with a start, noticed everyone applauding, and joined in.

Then Benjamin did the Amazing Guillotine trick, with Aunt Yetta being the volunteer finger. She was a very good sport, Aunt Yetta was, but the rest of the audience was quite nervous that Aunt Yetta was about to be separated from her very nice finger which had been with her for all of her eighty-two years. There were cries of "Benjamin, you don't know what you're doing" and "Stop it, Benjamin, what if something goes wrong?" Well, that was a question, but Aunt Yetta's finger was already in the guillotine and Benjamin, The Amazing Benjamin, was a magician after all, so he pushed down on the blade with a flourish.

Thankfully, the trick blade went around Aunt Yetta's finger as it was supposed to, and then it neatly cut the cigarette in half. There was an audible exhaling of breath from the various family members—it sounded like a steam pipe going off. Then everyone applauded and Benjamin bowed deeply.

Benjamin then did his final trick, the colored handkerchiefs—there was much oohing and aahing as each handkerchief magically changed colors before everyone's eyes. For his closer, Benjamin mimed his new favorite song, *Smoke Gets in Your Eyes* by The Platters.

After the show, Grandpa Gelfinbaum said, "If he's such a magician, why doesn't he make himself disappear?"

Grandma Gelfinbaum turned to her husband and said, "Oh, why don't you go to the toilet and while you're there you should only fall in."

"Listen to how she talks to me," Grandpa Gelfinbaum said to a roomful of people who were not listening to him.

Ernie got up and turned on the television so they could all watch *The $64,000 Question*. Minnie brought in a plate with vanilla and chocolate macaroons on it. Benjamin took one of each and retired to his room, where he removed his The Amazing Benjamin outfit (cape—well, a sheet pretending to be a cape—top hat, and fake moustache), turned on his transistor radio and pulled out his book of Connect the Dots pictures. Benjamin loved Connect the Dots pictures—only he didn't connect the dots the way you were supposed to, he connected them randomly, thereby turning the pictures into something totally weird and peculiarly Benjaminesque. Many of his pictures took on the strange appearance of vegetables gone awry. He liked to think of them as Benjamin's Mutant Vegetables—and he gave them names like the Cucado, the Stringpeas, the Squashroom, and his favorite, the Tomatochoke. Yes, Benjamin was very fond of his mutant vegetable Connect the Dots pictures, and he displayed them proudly on his bulletin board.

*   *   *

One day, Benjamin was sitting in his sixth grade classroom, and his teacher, the nice but bland Mrs. MacDonald, was droning on about things geographical—of course, things geographical put Benjamin right to sleep. She was talking about where countries in Europe were located, and was currently talking about Switzerland. Benjamin was doodling on a piece of notebook paper, and when Mrs. MacDonald said "Switzerland," Benjamin wrote it down. He looked at it curiously, crossed out the "Sw" and replaced it with a "Kr" and voilá, suddenly it said Kritzerland.

Kritzerland—Benjamin loved that. With just a tiny switch in letters, he'd invented his very own actual country. He began to think of what it would be like in Kritzerland. A country where everything would be the way he wanted it to be. Right then and there he decided the official food of Kritzerland would *not* be brisket. No, it would be a Fosters Freeze cheeseburger (his new favorite, since Kentucky Boys had closed its doors). That was a fine official food. The official dessert would be a Helms chocolate donut. In Kritzerland, everyone would use spelled-backwards words—for example, instead of being a citizen, a person would be a nezitic. And any nezitic who didn't play by the rules would be banished to Airebis. Just like money had an official motto ("In God We Trust") so Kritzerland would have an official motto: "What Is It, Fish?"

As soon as school let out, Benjamin rushed home so he could start a Kritzerland section in the Word Notebook. What a wonderful thing this was going to be—his own country where he was in charge, a country he could escape to when he got tired of being around his mutant brother, and his Martian parents. If only he'd had the foresight to invent Kritzerland when Susan was around—she could have run away with him to Kritzerland and they could have lived happily-ever-after.

On Saturday, Benjamin ran to Leo's Delicatessen for his morning soda pop and he told Leo about Kritzerland. Leo wanted to be the first to sign up to be an official nezitic, and they toasted the new country with Canada Dry Ginger Ale and a pickle from the pickle barrel.

Kritzerland, home of the evarb and the eerf. Benjamin loved his new country, and late at night he'd lie in bed, covers pulled over him, transistor radio on, while he imagined what it would be like to live in Kritzerland, forever and ever.

CHAPTER THREE

Clutch Cargo, Pig Latin, and Leaving Crescent Heights

One day, when Benjamin was home sick with a cold, he was watching *Sheriff John's Lunch Brigade*. Minnie had just made him some chicken noodle soup and Benjamin was shlurping it from the bowl when Sheriff John said they were about to show a brand new cartoon in a brand new kind of process, which they'd then be running every day on his show. The cartoon was called *Clutch Cargo* (with his pals, Spinner and Paddlefoot).

As it began, there was a shot of Clutch and friends from far away—with Clutch Cargo looking like a typical square-jawed hero from any number of cartoons. But when it went to a closer view, suddenly Benjamin could see that the cartoon Clutch had a *real* mouth. So did his friends. Everyone in the cartoon had real mouths. Benjamin sat

41

there in bed, with a noodle hanging out of his mouth, not believing what he was seeing. Why did these cartoon characters have real mouths? That was just too weird for Benjamin—that just gave Benjamin the willies. Whose brilliant idea was this, that's what Benjamin Kritzer wanted to know? Who had actually thought, "I know, let's do a cartoon but with real mouths." Benjamin couldn't understand the *point*; he simply could not make sense of what he was seeing. And yet, he could not stop watching Clutch, with his real mouth in his cartoon face. Like his mutant vegetable drawings, this was like a mutant *cartoon*, he thought. There was a girl in the cartoon, too, and she had a real mouth. But how could he be sure that the girl's real mouth was even a girl? After all, you could put a boy's mouth in a girl's cartoon face and who would be the wiser? He sat there, absolutely hypnotized by *Clutch Cargo*.

When the show was over, Minnie came in to collect the soup bowl and asked him how he was feeling. Benjamin replied, using exaggerated lip movements like the real mouths in the *Clutch Cargo* cartoon. "I'm feeling a little better, Mother. Thank you for asking." Minnie just looked at her son and finally said, "What did I do to deserve this?" and walked out of the room shaking her head back and forth like the pendulum in the dining room clock.

That night, Benjamin had a horrible dream. In his dream, he was on the school playground, and all the kids were pointing at him and laughing and making fun of him. He checked to make sure his zipper was up, checked to make sure he was even dressed (he frequently had dreams where he found himself naked in public)—well, his zipper was up and he was dressed, so what on earth were they laughing at him for? He ran away from them, ran into the building and into the boys' room. He turned toward the mirror across from him and saw the same old Benjamin. He walked closer to the mirror and then he saw what the problem was. He had a cartoon mouth. His eyes widened and he began to scream, his scream coming from deep within that awful cartoon mouth.

He woke up, screaming out loud. He looked over to Jeffrey, who was still sound asleep. Benjamin got up and went into the bathroom. He closed the door, turned on the light and walked over to the mirror. His eyes widened in horror—he still had a cartoon mouth. He started screaming again.

He woke up, this time for real. He was sweating and his heart was pounding. He looked over to Jeffrey who was sound asleep. Far off in the distance, he could hear the sound of sirens—it seemed there were always sirens going off in the middle of the night somewhere. He put his fingers up to his mouth and felt it. It was his real mouth. Of course it was his real mouth; real boys didn't have cartoon mouths. Still, it had been a terrible dream, and had probably even been exacerbated by his fever. He sneezed twice, blew his nose and went back to sleep, trying not to think of Clutch Cargo and Spinner and Paddlefoot and their cartoon faces with real mouths. Of course, he had to watch some more *Clutch Cargo* cartoons the next day.

* * *

A few weeks later, Benjamin was sitting in the den watching The Three Stooges, munching on a Snickers. Minnie walked in and grabbed the half-eaten candy bar from him and said, "Hey, ixnay on the andycay. You won't have any room for dinner. We're having Spenser steak." There were so many things wrong with that sentence that Benjamin just sat there with an unchewed mouthful of Snickers, looking at his mother. First of all, why did Spenser have a steak named after him? For example, why wasn't it Gregory steak or Steve steak? But he ignored that and got right to the most important thing.

"Ixnay on the andycay?" he said, chewing away at the Snickers.

"Yes, ixnay on the andycay. Don't look at me like that, you know what it means, Benjamin. It's Pig Latin."

"Pig Latin?"

"You've heard Pig Latin before, Benjamin, don't pretend you haven't," Minnie said, with exasperation. "You have to make such a thing out of everything. It's Pig Latin, plain and simple."

"Pig Latin, plain and simple," Benjamin said, swallowing the Snickers in a gulp.

"Yes, Benjamin, igpay atinlay."

He just stared at her.

"It's like talking to a brick wall, why do I bother?" Minnie said, sighing loudly as she went back into the kitchen, presumably to attend to Spenser's steak.

Benjamin finished watching The Three Stooges (he'd seen many of these shorts at the Picfair with Grandpa Kritzer, but they'd recently started showing them on Channel 11, and he absolutely loved them), went to the bookshelf and got down the "P-Q" volume of the *Encyclopedia Britannica* and went to his room. He looked up "Pig Latin" but there was nothing there. What good was the *Encyclopedia Britannica*, when it didn't even have a section on Pig Latin? Benjamin decided right then and there to write his own encyclopedia, the Benjamin Kritzer Encyclopedia of Strange Things. Pig Latin would be the first entry, he decided. He got a few pieces of lined paper from his notebook and went to work. He worked studiously (much more studiously than he did on his homework) for an hour, then ate Spenser's steak, salad and boiled potatoes, then went back to his room to studiously work some more. He worked for two more solid hours on his history of the origin of Pig Latin—but since he had no clue as to the real origin of Pig Latin, he simply made up his own. After he was finished, he proudly surveyed his handiwork. His writing was very neat and his first entry in the Benjamin Kritzer Encyclopedia of Strange Things looked quite excellent, if he did say so himself, which he did.

PIG LATIN EXPLAINED
By Benjamin Kritzer

Pig Latin was invented by Jerome Nussbaum, a science professor and lover of pigs. One fine day Mr. Nussbaum was out in the yard, speaking to his pigs. He always spoke to his pigs in Latin, for reasons that were only clear to Mr. Nussbaum. While he was speaking Latin to the pigs, the pigs would look Mr. Nussbaum squarely in the eye, as if to say, "What in the name of pork are you talking about?" These pigs apparently didn't give a fig or even a Fig Newton for Latin. No, these pigs were not interested in Latin, although they did like to do the cha-cha. So, there he was, speaking Latin to the pigs, when one of the pigs went up to Mr. Nussbaum and pooped on his shoe. This took Mr. Nussbaum aback. This flabbergasted Mr. Nussbaum and all he could think of to say was, "Hey, what's with the ooppay on the oeshay?" Suddenly the pigs sat up (not easy for a pig), and looked at Mr. Nussbaum with all their attention. This was a language they could understand. Mr. Nussbaum saw this and said, "Igpays, you ikelay the igpay atinlay?" to which the pigs responded with a grunt, which Mr. Nussbaum took as a rousing esyay. And so, Pig Latin was born. Mr. Nussbaum went on to win the Nobel Pig Prize for having come up with a language that pigs could finally understand. So, to Mr. Nussbaum we can only say: Anksthay to ouyay.

THE END

Benjamin put his entry on Pig Latin into his Word Notebook for safe keeping. The next day he would buy a new notebook, specifically for his brand new Encyclopedia of Strange Things.

* * *

Benjamin got a new teacher, Mrs. Haverty, for his final semester at Crescent Heights Elementary School. Mrs. Haverty seemed very nice and she didn't give a lot of homework, so Benjamin liked her very much.

An entire phase of his life was coming to an end because in June he would be graduating from grammar school and entering Louis Pasteur Junior High School. That made Benjamin very apprehensive (as did any major change from his normal everyday life) and he tried not to think about it. It was going to be a whole different world—Jeffrey had told him stories of junior high school and Benjamin didn't like the stories, therefore Jeffrey told him more stories and the less Benjamin liked them the more Jeffrey told him.

For example, in junior high school you had a different teacher for every class. You went from classroom to classroom—in other words, there was no one room you could call your own. Then there was the little matter of Gym class. Benjamin did not like the sound of Gym class. Jeffrey had told him that every day he was going to have to go to Gym class—to change in front of everyone and exercise and play sports and wear what Jeffrey called a jockstrap. Benjamin had seen Jeffrey's jockstrap and had almost thrown up—why would anyone wear such a contraption? It had no back, your rear end just hung out there like so much fish—what was the point of *that*? And Benjamin did not like sports, did not like to exercise, did not want to play football or baseball or basketball or volleyball, and most certainly Benjamin did not want to undress and dress in front of a lot of strangers.

Oh, this junior high school business sounded frightening, there was no question about it. And Benjamin Kritzer knew from frightening and he didn't like frightening. The Bad Men were frightening and he hated the Bad Men, even though they weren't around much these days. *House on Haunted Hill,* which he'd recently seen, had been frightening. Yes, Benjamin Kritzer knew from frightening, and the thought of wearing one of those jockstrap contraptions and dressing and undressing in front of strangers paralyzed him with fear.

As the weeks went by, Benjamin's fears about junior high school grew worse and worse. He began to think maybe he should do something so he wouldn't graduate. After all, he was used to Crescent Heights, Crescent Heights had been his world since the first grade. But come September he would be facing the unknown. As if the stories of Gym class and jockstraps weren't enough, Jeffrey continued to torment him, this time with terrifying stories of Wood Shop. Just the name Wood Shop made Benjamin want to vomit on the ground. Jeffrey, with great relish, told him tales of kids who'd mangled their fingers using the electric saw while making their Wood Shop projects, and told him about Mr. Godowski, the Wood Shop teacher, who was known to hurl erasers at students he didn't think were doing a good job. Benjamin was petrified, Benjamin was mortified, Benjamin was every kind of "fied" that a person could be, because he was quite certain he would not be doing a good job in Wood Shop and therefore Mr. Godowski would be pelting him with erasers every day.

* * *

School days came and went, weekends came and went, Benjamin came and went, usually to the movies, to Index Records and Radio to buy the latest 45s (the rotund and sweet Mrs. Index always kept the latest 45s and EPs in a special place behind the counter—the Benjamin stack—so he could see them first), to Leo's Delicatessen for his soda pops and pickles and good conversation, to Marty's Bike and Candy Shop for his red licorice, to Big Town Market for his pizza slices, and to the magic shop at Pacific Ocean Park (he'd recently purchased a Hypo-Phony—a trick hypodermic syringe—when you stuck the needle in an arm and pulled up, it revealed red, as if blood were being withdrawn).

Then there were his frequent sojourns to Daylight Market. It was there that he discovered two things that intrigued him no end. One was something called Flavor Straws. According to the package, when you put a Flavor Straw in a glass of milk and then sipped through it, suddenly the milk would be flavored. Since Benjamin hated milk with a passion, he thought Flavor Straws might just be a way to at least tolerate it. He saw two flavors on the shelf, chocolate and strawberry, and he asked Minnie to buy him some of the strawberry kind.

When he got home, he immediately went to the refrigerator and got out the milk carton and poured himself a glass of milk. He opened the package of Flavor Straws, put one into the glass and took a sip. While the Flavor Straw certainly did impart a hint of strawberry flavor (actually, it tasted like strawberry-flavored chalk), it could not disguise the milk flavor and therefore Benjamin went directly to the sink, spit it out, and then dumped the rest down the drain.

He was curious as to how the Flavor Straw worked, and so he cut one open. Inside was a little strip, which Benjamin presumed was a flavor strip. As the milk went through the straw it passed over the flavor strip on its way to the drinker's mouth. His curiosity satisfied, he put the Flavor Straws package into the cupboard, next to a package of Junket. The Junket Area, as Benjamin liked to think of it, was a little corner of the cupboard where things went that would never be used or eaten. For example, the package of Junket had been there since he was six. In fact, there were three packages of Junket, as well as two cans of Spam (Benjamin didn't want to have anything to do with anything named Spam), something called Bristling Sardines (what sane person would ever eat anything called Bristling Sardines?), a can of cocktail franks, and various other disgusting-looking cans and packages. And now the Flavor Straws joined the ranks of food in The Junket Area. Frankly, Benjamin would have rather had warts again than ever use one of those Flavor Straws, but, of course, that made perfect sense, since "straw" *was* "warts" spelled backwards. He went to his room and immediately made an entry for Flavor Straws in his Encyclopedia of Strange Things.

The other item he found at Daylight Market that intrigued him was a new product (Benjamin was always intrigued by new products) called Fizzies. They came in a variety of festive flavors like grape and cherry and orange and lime. And Fizzies didn't use milk, they used water. Fizzies were tablets and, according to the package, when you dropped one into an ordinary glass of water it fizzed up and flavored the water, and also carbonated the water, so it was like having a soda pop. Of course, one could just *buy* soda pop, so what the point of Fizzies was exactly eluded Benjamin. Still, he had to have a box, so Minnie dutifully bought him one, a variety pack with multiple flavors.

When he got home, Benjamin immediately filled up a glass with ice water from the ice water spigot attached to the side of the refrigerator and dropped a Fizzie tablet into it. The water immediately turned red (he'd used cherry flavor) and bubbled up, just like an Alka-Seltzer. Actually, two years prior, when Benjamin had eaten something that was far too rich for him and was feeling nauseous, Minnie had given him an Alka-Seltzer—she told him that by drinking that disgusting-looking liquid his tummy would feel all better. So, he drank it, drank it all down in one big gulp, just as Minnie told him to, only it was so vile and awful-tasting that it hadn't made his tummy all better—in fact, he'd thrown up immediately, right there on the kitchen floor. So much for ever taking an Alka Seltzer again.

In any case, the way the Fizzie bubbled up reminded him of the way the Alka Seltzer had bubbled up, only the Fizzie was bubbling up bright red. He took a sip, and was pleasantly surprised; it was pretty good. It wasn't as good as real soda pop, but then again it didn't cost as much as real soda pop and there was no bottle to return either. He downed the rest of his Fizzie in one long gulp. It was sparkling, he thought—a sparkling drink. He then tried the grape—he dropped the tablet into another glass of ice-cold water and this time the water turned purple as it bubbled up. He took a big gulp and the grape was even more sparkling than the cherry. He took the glass outside and drank the rest of it while playing in Ernie's Ford (Benjamin loved sitting behind the wheel of Ernie's Ford and pretending he was driving, chasing criminals like Broderick

Crawford on *Highway Patrol*). The Fizzies got to stay in the good part of the cupboard, nowhere near The Junket Area and the Flavor Straws.

* * *

Crescent Heights Elementary School was having a Graduation Day for Benjamin's class—the ceremony would be held in the auditorium and each graduating class member's name would be read aloud while they stood up (the entire class would be seated in chairs on the tiny stage). Graduation was still two weeks away, but they rehearsed for it several times.

Benjamin was trying to convince Minnie and Ernie not to come, but they weren't having any of it. Benjamin had actively begun to hate being anywhere with his parents— Ernie would fall asleep at the drop of a hat, and Minnie would pick at Benjamin, straightening his shirt and smoothing down his hair and telling him to stand up straight—a never-ending litany of fussing, mussing and talking, and it was all too embarrassing for words.

* * *

Graduation Day finally arrived. Benjamin was neatly dressed, hair combed (Minnie had even put "a little dab'll do ya" of Brylcreem in it to give it that special sheen), and totally uncomfortable in hard black shoes. He was currently seated in Mrs. Haverty's classroom, and she was telling everyone how proud she was of them and how she'd miss each and every one of them when they left. Of course, Benjamin couldn't imagine that she'd actually miss Hershey

53

Miller, with his obnoxious braying laugh and his habit of loudly breathing up snot through his nose and then swallowing it. Certainly *Benjamin* was not going to miss Hershey Miller, although, he supposed, he might have to be in a class with him in junior high school.

Then Mrs. Haverty was telling everyone to have a wonderful summer and to have a wonderful future. She then had everyone rise and get in a line and off they marched to the auditorium. The class entered through the rear door and was led on stage, where they all sat down in their assigned chairs. The parents were already seated in the auditorium, and they applauded as the sixth grade classes took their seats. Benjamin could already see Minnie and Ernie, because Minnie was waving at him with great gusto from the first row. She had to sit in the first row? She had to wear a gold puffy dress that could be seen for three blocks? Ernie's head was lolling dangerously, which meant that any minute he'd be snoring loudly. What could a child of eleven do with such parents?

Mrs. Peck, the principal of Crescent Heights Elementary School, got up and went to the podium, where she made a very nice speech. Then, each child who was in the graduating class had their name called and each stood up and remained standing while the other names were called. Finally, they called Benjamin's name and he stood up. He could see Minnie punch Ernie on the arm and Ernie waking with a start and smiling as if he'd never been asleep. It took another fifteen minutes to call the rest of the names, then Mrs. Peck congratulated the class and wished them well in all their future endeavors. The parents once again applauded loudly and the sixth grade class whooped and hollered noisily. Suddenly students were running into the auditorium and parents were coming up on stage and the whole place was a madhouse.

Benjamin wanted to quietly escape, but there they were, Minnie and Ernie, lumbering up to the stage. Minnie hugged Benjamin and so did Ernie. Benjamin believed that the only reason they did such a thing was because the other parents were doing such a thing. Minnie and Ernie never hugged the brothers Kritzer in their very own home, and kisses between the Kritzers were practically non-existent. Yet there was Minnie, kissing Benjamin on the cheek, leaving a big red lipstick stain.

Benjamin told his parents that he had to say goodbye to his schoolmates and that he wanted to say goodbye to Mrs. Wallett, the teacher he'd had for fourth grade. Since it was one o'clock, Ernie had to get back to his restaurant, the Erro, before the lunch crowd was totally gone, and Minnie told Benjamin they'd celebrate later by going out to a special dinner at Lawry's Restaurant, Home of the Prime Rib. And then Minnie and Ernie were thankfully and mercifully gone.

Benjamin didn't really have too many goodbyes to say, for he'd be seeing most of his schoolmates come September and, if truth be told, he wasn't really close with any of them anyway. He left the auditorium and walked across the schoolyard to the bungalow where Mrs. Wallett's classroom was located.

She was there, packing up a box, sweater over her shoulders, as always. She looked up and saw Benjamin standing at the door, and smiled.

"Well, how does it feel—going off to junior high school already? My goodness."

Benjamin entered the room and went over to her.

"I just wanted to tell you that you were my favorite teacher. I won't ever forget you."

Mrs. Wallett stood there, a book in mid-air on its way to the box, genuinely taken aback.

"Why, Benjamin Kritzer, what a nice thing to say. And I won't forget you either—you are a wonderful and very special boy."

She hugged him, and he felt such warmth from her, the kind of warmth he never ever felt from his parents, and he simply didn't want to let go. She gave him a kiss on the top of his head. He hung around the room for a few more minutes, helping her pack the box and then said goodbye.

He went to the lunch court and looked at the bench near the sandbox. It was the same bench that Susan Pomeroy had been sitting on two years ago, when he'd first laid eyes on her. He could practically see her there—her blonde hair and her incredible smile and her adorable voice saying, "Hello, Benjamin Kritzer, 4th grade, Mrs. Wallett's class, I'm Susan Pomeroy, 4th grade, Mrs. Bledsoe's class." Those simple words had opened up a whole new world to Benjamin Kritzer; a world of happiness, and fun, and closeness, and yes, even love. But Susan Pomeroy wasn't on the bench, and he hadn't seen or heard from her in over two years since she'd moved to Canada.

Benjamin stood there for awhile, then walked over to the gate where Susan and he always met after school. He looked across the schoolyard, which was now totally empty and silent. He turned around and walked out the gate, leaving behind Crescent Heights Elementary School and a part of his life forever.

CHAPTER FOUR

The Beginning of Summer

B enjamin loved summertime. There was no school, he could sleep late (well, until ten o'clock anyway), watch lots of daytime television (for some reason he'd become obsessed with a show called *Queen for a Day*, where some downtrodden woman would get everything she wanted for one day, after which, one supposed, she'd go back to being downtrodden again), play in the yard, run around the neighborhood and visit all his favorite haunts.

Every day when the postman would arrive, Benjamin would run to the mailbox because there would always be an envelope or two for him. That was because for the last three months he'd been sending for tickets to television shows. He'd amassed quite a wonderful collection of them—they were all different colors and very impressive and important looking. He had tickets to *The Jack Benny*

Show, To Tell the Truth, Art Linkletter's House Party, The Danny Thomas Show—not that he ever used the tickets; he wasn't old enough to go by himself and he certainly didn't want to go with his parents. He just liked sending for them and receiving them in an envelope with his name on it and the return addresses of CBS, or NBC, or ABC.

On days when he wasn't at home or running around the neighborhood, he went with Ernie to the Erro. But first Ernie would have to stop at the two bars he owned to get the previous day's receipts. They'd drive east on Pico; as they'd pass La Brea, the neighborhood just got seedier and seedier as they made their way towards Western. Somewhere in the last year or two, Ernie had picked up Grandpa Gelfinbaum's smoking-cigars-and-spitting habit. It wasn't bad enough having the Ford suffused with ugly-smelling cigar smoke, no, that was not enough. Every two or three blocks Ernie would suddenly pull over, stop, open his driver's side door, hock a big glob of spit on the ground, close the door and drive on. Benjamin hated the cigar smell and hated the hocking, but what could he do about it, other than try to ignore it, which was not easy when it happened every two blocks.

Along the way, Benjamin would watch for the various movie theaters he'd never been to—the Del Mar and the Midway, although they were both really tiny-looking and unappealing (from the front at least), so he didn't really care whether he'd been to them or not—and he'd look for the big Sears store on the south side of Pico, because next to it was where they kept all the out-of-service buses for the city. There were hundreds of them, all lined up next to each other—it was quite a sight to see and Benjamin thought it would be such fun to play on them.

Then they'd pass a huge Roman-looking building on Pico and Norton, and that was Benjamin's favorite. It was called the Forum, and once upon a time it had been a grand palace of a movie theater. Not only had it been a grand palace of a movie theater, but it also had a grand ballroom and apparently it had been a truly spectacular place in its day. Ernie had told Benjamin stories about the Forum and Benjamin wanted so much to go inside the Forum and look around and see that grand palace of a movie theater and ballroom. But he couldn't, because the Forum was all boarded up and had been closed for years. Benjamin wanted his father to buy the Forum for him, and Ernie would puff on his cigar and say, "Maybe someday, maybe someday."

A block from there was Ernie's bar, The Starlight. It was on the north side of Pico, so Ernie would have to turn left and swing the car around so he could park in front of it. Benjamin would go inside, because the bartender always had the discard 45s from the big Wurlitzer jukebox for him. Benjamin hated the smell in these bars; they were dark and musty and dank, and thoroughly depressing. After he'd get his handful of 45s, and while Ernie was getting the receipts and cash, Benjamin would go next door to the Peter Pan market to look around. Any market called Peter Pan was okay with Benjamin, because he loved Peter Pan (the market had a huge Peter Pan image on its sign)—he loved Peter Pan because Peter Pan could fly, just like Superman could fly, and, of course, Benjamin wanted to fly, too, to soar above the skies with not a care in the world. He'd already decided that everyone would be able to fly in Kritzerland.

After Ernie was through at the Starlight (the whole business didn't even take ten minutes), they'd head over to Ernie's other bar, the Satin Room, on Crenshaw near Olympic. It was the same routine there, and then they'd finally arrive at the Erro around eleven.

Benjamin would eat his maraschino cherries, drink his ginger beer, eat some shrimp cocktail shrimp from the barrel in the kitchen—all the things he'd always done. Then Ernie would let him use the big adding machine and he'd help Ernie total up the receipts. Benjamin hated anything to do with arithmetic but he did like punching the big number keys and pulling the lever on the side of the machine.

Then, at lunch time, Al, the chef, would make Benjamin a big turkey sandwich on white bread (with *very* light mayonnaise—if there was one thing Benjamin Kritzer hated it was mayonnaise that oozed out of a sandwich; that just made him want to vomit on the ground), and off he'd go to the Wiltern Theater to see a movie. Carrying his lunch in a brown paper bag, he'd walk west on 8th over to Western, then up Western, and there, just past Yaekel Brothers Oldsmobile, was the Wiltern, at Wilshire and Western.

Benjamin loved walking past Yaekel Brothers; there was always a television camera truck there because they broadcast live commercials from Yaekel Brothers. Of course, the television camera wasn't nearly as impressive as the huge VistaVision camera which was constantly filming the daily doings of Benjamin Kritzer, but still it was pretty impressive-looking. He'd peek into the truck as he walked by and he could see several small television screens in there, along with some interesting-looking controls and knobs and buttons. Benjamin was totally enamored of any controls or knobs or buttons, and he'd eye them and wish he could be in there pushing them and turning them.

The box-office at the Wiltern opened at noon and the first show began at 12:30. Benjamin, as was his wont, had to be first in line and he always was. He'd pay his fifty-cents, enter the theater and immediately go to the lounge which, unlike most of the theaters Benjamin went to, was downstairs rather than upstairs. That was just fine, because that meant he could roll down the stairs *first* rather than wait until after he'd used the bathroom. The lounge at the Wiltern was spectacular, almost as big as the entire front of the Kritzer house. They had sofas and chairs and a gorgeous patterned burgundy rug, and there were pillars and there was a fireplace; off to one side was a door that led to the men's room. Benjamin thought that a person could live down in the lounge very comfortably.

After visiting the lounge, Benjamin would go back upstairs, enter the dimly-lit auditorium, go down the left center aisle and find his tenth-row seat. On the off-chance someone had gotten to it before him, he simply gave them a quick dose of The Halb Treatment and they were quickly on their merry way to another seat. As soon as the cartoons and coming attractions began, Benjamin would unwrap his turkey sandwich with light non-oozing mayonnaise and he'd eat it slowly while the cartoon and coming attractions would unveil.

On one particular June afternoon, they were showing a movie called *Hercules*. Benjamin had been looking forward to *Hercules* because the advertisements for it were so bold and colorful and huge. It was a strange movie and Benjamin liked it very much. It had big men in little dresses, which he found amusing. Hercules himself was like that guy Charles Atlas who was in those "ninety-eight-pound weakling" ads. He had incredibly big muscles and no one but no one fooled around with Hercules, and if they did he would throw a big boulder on them. The women in the film were very pretty and wore gowns you could practically see through. Gowns you could practically see through were always fine with Benjamin. The other thing that Benjamin found interesting about *Hercules* was that the actors' mouths never seemed to be forming the words that were actually coming out of them.

When Benjamin got home that afternoon, he went to the bathroom and got a towel. He then went to his closet and took off his clothes (except for his underpants), wrapped the towel around him and looked in the mirror. He did not resemble Hercules but he stood there anyway, pretending he did. He walked around the bedroom, doing Hercules poses, then he went out in the yard and walked around to where the incinerator was, in back of the garage. That area of the yard hadn't been used for years, but it was filled with gravel and rocks. Benjamin picked up several rocks as if they were boulders, straining as if they weighed hundreds of pounds. He threw them down with great effort and pretended they were landing on Sandy Betleman, the bully of Sherbourne Drive, whom he despised. He continued playing in the yard until he heard Minnie's voice yelling, "Benjamin, what on earth are you doing in the yard in a towel? Get in the house and put some clothes on right now! What did I do to deserve such a child?"

* * *

When he wasn't going with Ernie to the Erro or seeing movies at the Wiltern, and when he wasn't watching *Queen for a Day* or running around the neighborhood, Minnie would sometimes try to coerce Benjamin to come with her to the beauty parlor with the promise of lunch at Ontra Cafeteria. Ever since Ontra Cafeteria had opened its doors, the Kritzers had become regular patrons. There were several locations—the Kritzers frequented two of them: one on Beverly Drive in Beverly Hills (Benjamin's favorite) and one on Wilshire in the Miracle Mile, very close to Orbach's department store.

The promise of lunch at Ontra Cafeteria was about the only thing Minnie could offer that would get Benjamin to go anywhere with her. *Why* she liked to have Benjamin with her when she went to the beauty parlor was a mystery. But Benjamin rather liked the beauty parlor—he liked the woman who did Minnie's hair (her name was Dorothy), because she was always very nice to him. He was usually the only young person there—otherwise it was all women getting their hair done, getting their nails done, and some even getting their toenails done.

The smell was peculiar, Benjamin thought, very pungent and not exactly pleasant but not exactly unpleasant either. He would sit there and look at these women, talking away endlessly, having their hair washed and combed and cut, then having ugly curlers put in, then sitting under those weird bubble-shaped hair dryers—and he would wonder why anyone would want to have their hair "done". Benjamin, for example, was perfectly content not to have his hair "done". If that was what one had to go through then Benjamin Kritzer was perfectly fine with his hair being "undone".

63

He'd watch as Dorothy would wash Minnie's hair and then rinse out the shampoo. He'd watch as she'd cut and shape the hair (and sometimes put foul-smelling goop in it—hair dye, Dorothy told him in secret), and then he'd watch as Dorothy put those ugly metal curlers in Minnie's hair. Then Minnie would go and sit under the hair dryer for quite some time, where she'd gab with all the other ladies under the other hair dryers. Benjamin had to admit that he was fascinated by those hair dryers—they were like things you'd see in science fiction movies. So, Benjamin would also sit under a hair dryer, even though he wasn't having his hair "done", and Dorothy would turn the dryer on for him. He'd feel the warm air coming from the big plastic hood, and he imagined he looked like something out of that movie, *This Island Earth*.

After Minnie was finished, her hair would be very full, high up in the air and sprayed to within an inch of its life so that if a sudden hurricane occurred Minnie's hair would stay just where it was and not move one inch. Benjamin thought he could probably bounce a ball off her hair, that's how hard the hairspray made it.

Then, with her hair "done", she and Benjamin would drive the few blocks to Beverly Drive, find a place to park and go to Ontra Cafeteria. They'd had quite a few arguments about how to pronounce the name Ontra. Minnie pronounced it "On-truh" and so did Ernie and so did Jeffrey. That was just ridiculous to Benjamin. It was a cafeteria, you put your food on a tray; therefore, the obvious pronunciation was "On-tray". But Minnie would have none of it, it was "On-truh" and that was all there was to it.

They walked in the front door and approached the line where people were standing. They got their trays, and started down the long row where the food was. Benjamin wanted everything. He wanted a fruit cup (even though he didn't love fruit), he wanted a bowl of cottage cheese (even though he didn't love cottage cheese), he wanted rolls, he wanted macaroni and cheese, he wanted turkey, he wanted mashed potatoes and gravy, he wanted peas (even though he hated peas, he thought they were amusing-looking), he wanted five different desserts. Minnie looked at his ever-mounting array of food and said, "Benjamin, stop it, your eyes are bigger than your stomach."

Benjamin looked over at Minnie slowly, making his eyes as big as he could, and said, "My eyes are bigger than my stomach?"

"You know what I mean—you'll never be able to eat that much food because your eyes are bigger than your stomach."

Benjamin thought about it for a moment. "If my eyes are bigger than my stomach, wouldn't my eyes take up my entire face? What would happen to my nose and my mouth?"

"Benjamin, shut up, don't embarrass me in the Ontra Cafeteria." Of course, she pronounced it "On-truh."

"On-tray. On-tray Cafeteria," Benjamin said loudly.

"No, Benjamin, it's On-truh," Minnie said with a sharp tone.

"Well, I guess my food is on a tray, and yours is on a truh," Benjamin replied.

"Benjamin, ixnay with the alktay, you're annoying me. This cafeteria is called On-truh and I don't want any more arguments from you or you will not be watching television this evening."

That was enough to shut Benjamin up, but he added a plate of Jell-O to his already crowded tray, just to further annoy Minnie. They made their way to the cashier and Minnie paid. Benjamin lifted his tray and Minnie lifted her truh, and they looked for a table. Minnie saw an empty table for two and said, "Hurry, Benjamin, go get that table." Benjamin hurried over to it and just in the nick of time because an elderly woman with pink hair was trying to make her way over to it. When she saw Benjamin set down his tray, the lady with the pink hair scowled at him and said something he couldn't hear.

Minnie sat down across from Benjamin and they started unloading their food plates off of their trays. As it turned out, Benjamin's eyes had indeed been bigger than his stomach because he could barely finish half his food. While Minnie finished her lunch, Benjamin made some food art— he put some Jell-O squares in the cottage cheese and then added a few peas and topped it with a bit of chocolate pudding. He called it Benjamin's Strange Mind.

CHAPTER FIVE

The Intruder, and Superman Is Dead

First there was tapping. Benjamin, deep in some dream or other, could faintly hear it. *Tap, tap, tap*. He turned over, now only half asleep. The tapping got louder and more insistent, and Benjamin suddenly woke with a start. He lay in bed, not moving, listening for the tapping. But there wasn't any tapping, just silence and the sound of crickets outside. He listened, to see if perhaps the Bad Men had come back and were rifling through the china cabinet like they used to, but he could hear nothing. It must have been the dream, he thought, somebody must have been tapping in his dream. He turned over, and as he did the tapping started again, only this time it was more like rapping than tapping. He whipped his head around and looked at Jeffrey, who was fast asleep. The rapping was coming from the window—someone was out there and they were rapping on the window. Benjamin froze—he could not move one inch. The rapping suddenly stopped, and then Benjamin could hear scratching noises. He cocked his head and looked over the table his bed was against, and up toward the window—someone was *opening* it, someone was opening his bedroom window. How could Jeffrey not hear this? The window was being nudged upward, and now Benjamin could see someone's hand. That was enough for Benjamin. He bolted from his bed, got out of the room and ran as fast as he could to his parents' bedroom.

He got there in about five seconds flat. Minnie and Ernie were, of course, fast asleep, and Ernie was snoring so loudly it sounded like canons going off. Breathlessly, Benjamin went to his mother's side of the bed and shook her, saying, "There's someone coming in through the window!"

Minnie's eyes shot open and she said, "What?" Benjamin could smell Listerine on her breath.

"Someone's breaking in the house. Someone's coming in through my window," Benjamin whispered.

Minnie immediately turned around and shoved Ernie, who woke with a snort and a start and said, "What's the matter?"

"Someone's trying to climb in the window in Benjamin's room," said Minnie, panic mounting in her voice.

"Someone's trying to climb in the window in Benjamin's room?" asked Ernie, who was sitting up. "When?"

Minnie smacked him. "When? *Now*, you big lummox. Go in there now!"

Ernie got out of bed quickly and put on his slippers. Benjamin looked at his father, standing there in a pajama top and nothing else and wondered what he needed the slippers for—wouldn't underpants or a robe be better? But Ernie was already on his way to the kids' bedroom, his ample behind jiggling as he walked, with Benjamin dogging his footsteps. As they left the room, Minnie said, "Be careful!"

Ernie, with Benjamin close behind, entered Benjamin and Jeffrey's bedroom in time to see the window half-open and an arm sticking in trying to reach Jeffrey. Ernie shouted, "Get out of here! We've called the police!"

By this time, Jeffrey had finally awakened. The intruding hand suddenly stopped intruding and withdrew quickly. Jeffrey was sitting up and saying, "It's okay, it's okay, don't call the police, it's just Jay."

Suddenly Jeffrey's best friend Jay's face appeared at the window. "Sorry, I was just trying to wake up Jeffrey— usually he gets right up when he hears me tapping."

There was silence and everyone just looked at each other. It was like some weird tableau: Ernie, standing there in only a pajama top and slippers; Benjamin, behind him, starting to laugh; Jeffrey, for once in his life not knowing what to say or do; and his best friend Jay, staring in the window with an innocent expression on his face, as if this nocturnal visit were the most natural thing in the world.

Jay finally broke the silence. "Well, I guess I'll be going now." He turned and ran off, his footsteps echoing as he padded across the driveway and down the street. Minnie, dressed in her quilted pink robe, entered the room. She looked at everyone, and said, "What on earth is going on here?"

No one quite knew what to say. Eventually, Ernie explained to Minnie what on earth was going on. Jeffrey explained to Minnie and Ernie (with Benjamin listening in) that he was running for a club and this visit was part of his initiation—apparently he had to meet everyone at two in the morning and drink a bottle of Ripple. Minnie asked what kind of club did such things, and Jeffrey replied the kind he was joining. Ernie told him that if anything like this ever happened again he would be punished for weeks and he wouldn't be allowed to be in the club—and if he was ever caught drinking Ripple he could be punished for years. By the time everyone got back into bed it was three in the morning. Benjamin was too keyed up to go back to sleep, and so was Jeffrey. After a minute, Jeffrey said, "Why did you have to go tell them, you big booger?"

"I thought it was a burglar or the Bad Men or a crazy person—how did I know? And don't call me a booger, you regoob," Benjamin replied, yawning while he said it.

"You are so stupid. What's a regoob?"

"If you don't know what a regoob is, how am I the one who's stupid, diputs?"

"Booger."

"Regoob."

"There is no such word as regoob, booger."

"Regoob is booger spelled backwards, regoob."

"You and your stupid backward words."

Benjamin was happy he was annoying his brother for a change. "Backwards words are not stupid, diputs."

"Diputs? What's a diputs?" Jeffrey asked.

"Diputs is stupid spelled backwards, diputs," Benjamin replied, giggling.

"Booger."

"Regoob."

"Stupid."

"Diputs."
Fifteen minutes later they were both sound asleep.

*   *   *

Over the next few nights, Benjamin began having a recurring nightmare that people were trying to get in through the window, and he'd awaken, thrashing about and yelling out loud for help.

*   *   *

Benjamin awoke on a sunny Tuesday morning in mid-June. He got up, dressed, ate his breakfast, and went out to do his neighborhood rounds. As Benjamin walked north on Sherbourne he could smell the honeysuckle which every other house seemed to have growing in their front yard.

He headed over to Index Records and Radio so he could buy his new favorite song, *Personality*, by Lloyd Price. Benjamin loved the main part of the song, and he'd already memorized the words, just from hearing it on the radio. He sang it aloud as he walked down Pico towards Shenandoah.

"Cause you've got personality
Walk, personality
Talk, personality
Smile, personality
Charm, personality
Love, personality
You've got a great big heart"

After all, Benjamin had always thought and continued to think that he was unique and special and that he reeked of personality. How could he not love a song called *Personality?*

He picked up the 45, then walked over to Big Town Market and had a slice of their delicious pizza pie. As always, the first bite seemed to burn the roof of his mouth, but he wolfed down the rest and had a small root beer as well.

Then he walked to the miniature golf course and played some of the games in their arcade. He stopped at Marty's Bike and Candy shop, got some red licorice, and then headed back home. As he walked by the building where Susan had lived, he thought of her, as he always did. By the time he got home it was already 2:30 in the afternoon.

Benjamin played his new 45 several times while he danced around his room to it, striking the various attitudes of the words in the song. He liked dancing around the room, making up steps and miming the words of whatever he was listening to, and he made up in energy what he lacked in dancing skills, which was plenty.

Benjamin went to the kitchen, looked around for a snack, and ended up on the porch taking a bite out of the hanging salami. He made a grape Fizzie and went into the den, turned on the television and watched *Mr. and Mrs. North* and *Lloyd Thaxton Record Shop*. Around four-thirty, Minnie came home and started cooking dinner. At five, Benjamin heard Ernie come in through the front door. As Ernie came into the den, he said hello to Benjamin and handed him the *Herald Express* so Benjamin could look at the movie section. Then Ernie went into his bedroom and closed the door.

Benjamin unfolded the newspaper and was about to discard the front section when he saw the headline. He stood there, the paper laid out on the sofa in front of him, and he stared at the headline in disbelief. It said: TV'S SUPERMAN ENDS LIFE. What did that mean? How could Superman be dead? Superman was the man of steel, able to leap tall buildings with a single bound, bullets bounced off his chest like ping-pong balls against a paddle—there was no way Superman could be dead. Benjamin had loved Superman on television since he was a little boy; he still had his Superman outfit and he still watched reruns of the show whenever they were on.

Benjamin found the article below the headline and read the story. Apparently, sometime after midnight, the actor who played Superman, George Reeves, had put a gun to his head and shot himself. Benjamin was smart enough to know that George Reeves wasn't really Superman, that he was an actor who played Superman, but still that didn't make it any easier to understand.

Benjamin left the paper there on the couch, went into his room and shut the door. He sat on his bed, motionless, trying to understand what he'd read. He didn't want Superman to be dead, it wasn't fair; the bullet never even should have hurt him. And yet, George Reeves, TV's Superman, was dead, because the bullet had not only hurt him, it had killed him.

After a while, Benjamin put on the *Guess Things Happen That Way* 45 and listened to Johnny Cash and the Tennessee Two sing forlornly:

I don't like it but I guess things happen that way

73

Later, Benjamin sat at the dinner table, picking at his lamb chops. Minnie looked at him and said, "Benjamin, is something wrong with you? Do you have a fever?" She felt his head, but it wasn't feverish. "Eat your lamb chops."

"I'm not hungry," Benjamin said, moving one of the lamb chops around on his plate with his fork.

Jeffrey swallowed his potato and said, "He's just upset because Superman killed himself."

Benjamin slammed his fork down on his plate, turned to Jeffrey and with some vehemence said, "Shut up!"

"Don't say 'shut up' at the table, Benjamin," Minnie said sternly.

"Fine." Benjamin got up from the table and went to the other side of the kitchen. "Shut up!" he said again, even louder. "Shut up, shut up, shut up!"

Ernie's tongue was starting to protrude, and he was turning red. "Shut up, Benjamin, and don't say 'shut up' anymore—you calm down or you're going to get a licking. You're being ridiculous!"

"I don't care! Why do I have to have a family like this? Why can't I have a family like *Leave it to Beaver* or *Ozzie and Harriet?* Why can't I have a normal family?" He was shouting now, uncontrollably. "He shouldn't be dead, why does he have to be dead?"

And with that, Benjamin ran from the kitchen to his room and slammed the door as loud as he could. He shut the light off and sat on his bed, his face red with anger. And quite suddenly, Benjamin Kritzer, the boy who didn't cry, was crying, crying for the first time since Susan had moved to Canada. Big sloppy tears poured down his cheeks and he couldn't stop them. He just sat there and wept because Superman was dead and if Superman was dead then there wasn't anything you could count on in the whole wide world.

His whole wide world was changing, and Benjamin hated change. He liked everything the way he liked it and he didn't see why it couldn't stay that way. He was never going to see Susan Pomeroy again, he was not going back to Crescent Heights Elementary School, he was about to enter the whole new world of junior high school and now Superman was dead.

He sat on his bed and dried his eyes. A little while later, Ernie came in and brought Benjamin some chocolate pudding, and told him to come watch television in the den. Benjamin said he'd be there in a little while. Ernie left the room and Benjamin ate his pudding, then pulled out his Word Notebook and turned to the Kritzerland section. That always made him feel better because Kritzerland was a happy place where Superman couldn't possibly be dead, where Susan Pomeroy and Benjamin would be holding hands and maybe even k-i-s-s-i-n-g, and where there were no Martian parents or psychotic brothers. Then he went to the den and watched *Wyatt Earp*.

CHAPTER SIX

The Dog Days of Summer, and The Four Stooges

Benjamin spent most of July going to the movies or going to Pacific Ocean Park. He'd seen some terrific pictures like *The Five Pennies* (he loved Danny Kaye, and the little girl who played Danny's daughter reminded him of Susan), *The Shaggy Dog,* and *The Mysterians,* and he'd clocked in more miles than he could possibly imagine on the Flight to Mars ride. In fact, he'd been on the Flight to Mars so many times that the people who worked that ride greeted him by name. Sometimes he'd walk north and go sit in the sand near the ocean and listen to the waves as they rolled ashore. He liked the smell and of course he also liked looking at the girls in their bathing suits.

Mr. Szymond at the magic shop would always show him the latest and greatest tricks and novelty items, and that was

76

always a highlight of his beach visits. Even though he didn't want to, he would always have to spend a little time with his grandparents. Grandma Gelfinbaum had taken to sitting downstairs in the lobby of the St. Regis, and when Benjamin would come back from his POP adventures, she'd always gesture him over and pinch him on the cheek really hard and say her usual "sheyne punim," and then introduce him to all her elderly friends. They'd always kvell and say things like, "What a handsome boy," "What a nice boy," "What a wonderful grandson," and all of that just made Benjamin want to vomit on the ground.

Grandpa Gelfinbaum was becoming more foul with each passing day. He'd sit in his chair watching *Search for Tomorrow* or *Love of Life* or whatever daytime serial was on, and if he didn't like what the characters in the show were doing, he'd yell at the television as if the people in the shows could hear him. When the commercials would come on he'd just sit there and say, "What is it, fish?" as every product paraded by. Benjamin couldn't take being in their apartment for very long, what with the smell of canned salmon and onions and Grandpa Gelfinbaum's ever-present smelly cigar, and his constant yelling at the television.

Benjamin needed something new and fun to do. Oh, he liked his routine, he thrived on his routine, but here it was, the middle of July and he was in the doldrums, whatever *they* were. He hadn't been aware that he'd been in the doldrums until Minnie had pointed it out to him, although she wasn't able to tell him exactly what the doldrums were. She did say he was in the doldrums because it was the dog days of summer. Benjamin didn't know what that meant either, and when he asked Minnie to explain it to him she just said, "Benjamin, stop being a pill."

Benjamin had no idea he was being a pill—he thought he was being a Benjamin. He wondered what kind of pill he was being—an aspirin, or maybe a One-a-Day Brand Multiple Vitamin? He also wanted to know the following: If there were dog days of summer did that mean there were cat days of winter? And bird days of fall?

Well, Benjamin the Pill, as he began to call himself, needed to do something new and fun to get himself out of the doldrums during the dog days of summer. The first new fun thing he did was to go into his parents' bathroom, take the can of baby powder from the medicine cabinet and pour it into his hair, turning his hair a chalky white color. Then he walked up to Pico and paraded down the street acting like Grandpa Gelfinbaum. That was fun and he got some very amusing looks from the passersby. Then he went into Big Town Market and ordered his usual slice of pizza pie, and, when it was handed to him, he said in his best Grandpa Gelfinbaum voice, "What is it, fish?" to which the uncomprehending pizza person had no reply.

The next new and fun thing Benjamin did was to take some of the red food dye from the kitchen cupboard and put it into a small plastic bag (the kind Minnie kept her current Five Day Deodorant Pad in). He waited until Wednesday when Lulu was cleaning the house. While she was doing the ironing, Benjamin casually walked into the room. He had the plastic bag with the red food dye cupped in his hand. He lifted the bag near his nose and then pretended to sneeze loudly, and at the exact same time he opened the plastic bag, causing the red food dye to stream forth, as if from his nose. Being a fine magician, he diverted attention from the plastic bag by making all manner of noises as the red food dye continued streaming down all over his mouth and chin. Lulu's eyes widened until they were as big as saucers. Before she could even open her mouth to say anything, Benjamin burst out laughing. Lulu put her hands on her hips and then shook a fist at Benjamin. "You little devil! You are gonna get your *be*hind swatted if you don't clean that mess up right now!" Then she began to howl with laughter too, and pretty soon the two of them were helplessly howling with laughter, tears streaming down their cheeks.

The next new and fun thing he did was to start going through all the drawers in his parents' bedroom. Ernie and Minnie had separate dressers—hers was very long and squat, with nine drawers, whereas Ernie's was tall with six drawers. There were also drawers at the foot of Minnie's closets. Benjamin found many items of interest in those drawers. He found at least ten small purses which all had things in them—old compacts, old lipsticks, he even found a dollar bill in one of them. He found an assortment of hats with veils attached, which he enjoyed trying on. He found a bundle of letters tied together. He removed one and opened it—it was from Ernie, but the writing was too hard to read and besides, Benjamin knew he shouldn't be reading it anyway, so he put the letter back in the bundle and returned it to the drawer he'd discovered it in. He also found a small gold box which contained a locket of hair. He wondered if it was Minnie's, from when she was young. He wondered why anyone would keep a locket of their long-ago hair. He found several jewelry boxes filled with earrings, the snap-on kind, and he tried those on too. When he was done going through Minnie's dresser drawers, he went into the bathroom, got out the small scissors and cut off a lock of his hair, which he put in an envelope and which he then put into the Benjamin Kritzer Encyclopedia of Strange Things; he labeled it "Benjamin Kritzer's Long-Ago Hair".

Next he went through Ernie's dresser drawers. He'd been through a few of them already, because he'd needed the cardboard from Ernie's laundered shirts for various projects. Benjamin found several interesting things in Ernie's dresser drawers—several pairs of old glasses, all of which Benjamin liked better than the big thick ugly black ones that Ernie currently wore. He found a couple of old driver's licenses, a pocket knife with a pearl handle, a wonderful old photo of Ernie as a child holding a violin, a few combs, and a box with cuff links and key chains in it. There was a deck of playing cards with scantily clad women on them, too, and Benjamin spent quite a lot of time looking at every card in the deck, and then going back through again to make sure he hadn't missed any.

He enjoyed doing all these new and fun things because they helped take his mind off the impending first day of junior high school. Even though it was still quite a few weeks away, Benjamin was filled with panic and absolutely terrified of starting his new school, and Jeffrey wasn't making it any easier. In addition to all the horrors he'd already instilled in Benjamin, like jockstraps and the eraser-throwing Wood Shop teacher, Jeffrey had added some new ones, including the fact that if a student got in trouble and got sent to the Vice Principal's office, he would be spanked with a wooden paddle as punishment. This was beginning to sound more like the prison camp in *The Bridge on the River Kwai* than junior high school, and the more diversions Benjamin found, the better.

*   *   *

Benjamin had loved The Three Stooges for as long as he could remember. He'd first seen their movies at the Picfair Theater, where they were shown every Saturday, along with the cartoons and the serial and the double feature. He loved all the Stooges—Larry, Moe and Curly, of course, but also Shemp and Joe Besser (he'd always liked Joe Besser, because he'd played Stinky in the *Abbott and Costello Show*—in fact, Benjamin did a pretty good impression of him saying his classic, "Ooh, I'm gonna *harm* you"). He loved the mayhem—the way Moe would poke the others in the eyes, the way he'd tear Larry's wild mane of hair from his head, and the way he'd slap Shemp or Joe. Moe was clearly the most malevolent of them, but he always got his, too. The Picfair had stopped showing the shorts during the last year and Benjamin missed them. But then, suddenly, there they were, every night on Channel 11. Benjamin never missed them and he quite liked the host of the show, Don Lamond, who seemed like a very nice person.

The television program had proven extremely popular and the Stooges found themselves with a whole new legion of fans. Joe Besser had retired, so they'd found a new person to replace him—Curly Joe DeRita was his name and he even sort of looked like the old Curly. They did public appearances together, and the whole television show had become so wildly successful that they'd rushed the Stooges into the studio to do their first feature-length film, *Have Rocket, Will Travel.*

Don Lamond had talked about the film and had even showed some clips from it on the show. Benjamin couldn't wait to see it and was just counting the days until it opened on August 19th.

About two weeks before *Have Rocket, Will Travel* was going to open, The Three Stooges were set to make an appearance and do a show at Frank Sennes' Moulin Rouge on Sunset Boulevard in Hollywood. Benjamin had seen that building many times (it was across the street from NBC Studios) and he'd even seen a photo of Minnie and Ernie sitting at a table in the fancy nightclub. Benjamin immediately went to Ernie and asked him if he would take him to see The Three Stooges in person at the Moulin Rouge. Ernie, never one to make a quick decision, said he'd think about it. Over the next few days, Benjamin never let up, bringing up the Stooges every five minutes, pestering Ernie as much as possible. Ernie played the whole thing close to his vest and wouldn't tell Benjamin whether he would take him or not.

Finally the day of the show arrived. Ernie suggested that Benjamin come with him to the Erro, but he simply wouldn't tell Benjamin whether or not he was taking him to see The Three Stooges. Benjamin moped around the restaurant, had a ginger beer and some maraschino cherries, and then ate some shrimp from the big barrel in the kitchen.

At one o'clock, Ernie came out of his office, glad-handed a few of the lunch patrons and made sure the lunch hour was going smoothly. He then found Benjamin and said, "Let's take a ride; I've got to do an errand." They got in Ernie's Ford and left the Erro parking lot. Ernie turned left onto 8th and drove west, then turned right onto Western and drove up to Sunset. By this point, Benjamin began to have a good feeling. He turned to Ernie and said, "Are we going where I think we're going?" His leg had started to go up and down a mile a minute.

"It's a nice day—I thought we'd drive into Hollywood and see what's happening," Ernie said, trying to suppress a smile.

They drove along, and the closer they got to Vine the more Benjamin's leg was behaving like one of the Harlem Globetrotters dribbling a ball. Suddenly, there on the left was Frank Sennes' Moulin Rouge. Ernie pulled into the parking lot. He turned to Benjamin and said, "I thought we'd go see The Three Stooges." As Benjamin got out of the car he said, "Thank you, thank you, thank you."

They entered the Moulin Rouge. It was huge. The inside was beautiful—it had black-and-white tiles on the floor just like the Kritzers had in their den, and there was a big bronze statue of a sort-of naked woman, which Benjamin liked very much. There were large columns and then tables, lots and lots of tables, tables as far as the eye could see, all covered with bright red tablecloths. Then, far from the back, where they were now standing, was a stage. Ernie was saying something to the maitre'd. Then they were led down to a table right in front of the stage. Benjamin couldn't believe it; this was the best table in the whole place. They sat down and Ernie said, "Good enough table?" Benjamin nodded his head affirmatively.

"One of my regular customers is a good friend of the man who runs this place," Ernie said. "Moe Atlas. You remember Moe Atlas?"

"Yes, Moe Atlas, he's nice," Benjamin answered. Of course, Moe Atlas had suddenly become Benjamin's favorite because he'd gotten them this front-and-center table to see The Three Stooges. But, as it turned out, that wasn't all Moe Atlas had arranged, no, not by a long shot.

About twenty minutes before the show was to start, the maitre'd came down the aisle and nodded at Ernie. Ernie turned to Benjamin and said, "C'mon, we've got to go meet some people." Benjamin couldn't imagine who they had to go meet, but figured it was just some friend of Moe Atlas' or Ernie's. They walked up the long aisle and were led to a door. The maitre'd knocked, the door was opened, and Ernie and Benjamin were led down a long corridor. They reached a large room with a sofa and chairs. Ernie and Benjamin were told to wait right there.

Benjamin looked across the room and he couldn't believe his eyes. For standing there, standing right there in front of him as big as life, were Larry, Moe and Curly Joe. Benjamin's mouth was practically on the floor. They were very short, as short as Ernie if not shorter. The maitre'd was saying something to them and then Curly Joe came over to where Benjamin and Ernie were standing. Curly Joe smiled and said, "Hi, Benjamin, thanks for coming to the show. I'm Curly Joe. We're gonna take a picture with you, how's that?"

How was that? That was great, that's how that was and Benjamin said so. Then Moe and Larry were walking over. They had very gruff, sour expressions on their faces. In a very gruff and terse tone, Larry said, "C'mon, let's get this over already, we've got to do a show." Moe chimed in, also tersely, "All right, put the kid in the middle and let's take the picture." Curly Joe winked at Benjamin and said, "Don't mind them, they're always like that." Curly Joe stood to Benjamin's left, then Larry, then Benjamin, then Moe. A photographer held his camera up, framed the shot, and suddenly Larry and Moe were all smiles. A flash went off as the photographer snapped the photo. Larry and Moe's smiles disappeared immediately and they walked away, but Curly Joe said, "Enjoy yourself, Benjamin—it was nice to meet you." Then Ernie and Benjamin were led back down the corridor, out the door and back to their front row table.

The place was now packed to the rafters with loud chattering children of all ages. Ernie leaned over to Benjamin and said, "Well, that should keep you happy until school starts. Then you can show everyone the photo and tell them you spent time with The Three Stooges." Benjamin nodded—it had been great even though Larry and Moe had been rather unfriendly. Benjamin looked around—hardly anyone had as good a table as he had, but then again the other kids' parents didn't know Moe Atlas.

The lights went down and the curtain opened. Without fanfare, the Stooges came on and the place went wild. The kids were screaming and whooping and hollering. The Stooges were on for an hour, and did all their poking and slapping and shoving and gouging, much to the delight of everyone in attendance, especially Benjamin, although he did notice that the poking and the slapping and the shoving and the gouging didn't have the same sounds they had in the movies, and therefore weren't quite as funny.

A week later, *Have Rocket, Will Travel* opened and Benjamin was there, first in line, at the opening show. It was at a theater he hadn't been to before, the Uptown, which was located at Olympic and Western, still close enough for Benjamin to walk to from the Erro. He was, of course, first in line and got in quickly and got his favorite seat. Within minutes, the theater was totally full. The

85

audience was practically all young kids and the din inside the theater was ear-shattering. The lights went down, and there was a cartoon and some coming attractions, but you couldn't hear the sound because the kids in the theater wouldn't shut up. This was very annoying to Benjamin, these rude kids—this was not a way to behave in a movie theater.

The film finally started, and still the kids would not shut up. About ten minutes later the film abruptly stopped and the manager of the theater came up on stage. He managed to quiet everyone down and he said, "If you rambunctious children don't stop this noise I will not show the film." That got a rather loud and vociferous "boo" from the crowd of rambunctious children, but then the manager just stood his ground and eventually the rambunctious children quieted down.

The movie resumed and the kids in the theater managed to remain well-behaved for the rest of it. Benjamin thought the movie was not nearly as funny as the shorts he'd seen at the Picfair or the ones they showed on television. Still, it wasn't bad, and Don Lamond, the host of the TV show even had a small part. The best part of the day was hearing the word "rambunctious". That was one of the stupidest-sounding words Benjamin had ever heard and he fell in love with it immediately. When he got home that afternoon, Minnie asked him how the movie was.

"Rambunctious," he said. He went to the den and got the big dictionary down from the bookshelf to look up the word "rambunctious". It took him quite a while to find it, because he assumed it was spelled the way it sounded—"rambunkshus". He eventually found it and not only was it one of the stupidest-*sounding* words he'd ever heard, it was also one of the stupidest-*looking* words he'd ever seen. "Rambunctious". There were so many useless letters in that word it wasn't even funny. According to the dictionary, it meant wild, disorderly, boisterous, unruly. Benjamin marveled at the word, and he wondered how anyone could have even come up with such a word and, having actually come up with it, have spelled it like that. Some word person or other had looked at someone behaving wildly and thought, "Oh, dear me, look at that wild behavior, I think I'll call that wild behavior 'rambunctious'." Well, it was one for the Word Notebook and he dutifully entered it, feeling very rambunctious as he did so.

A few days later, Ernie brought home the photo of Benjamin and The Three Stooges. There, in the photo, were Larry, Moe and Curly Joe all surrounding Benjamin and all smiling goofily; Benjamin looked like he'd been hit by a truck. He wrote on the back of the photo "The Four Stooges" and put it up on his bulletin board.

CHAPTER SEVEN

North by Northwest, and The End of Summer

One fine Wednesday, Benjamin went with Ernie to the Erro, so he could go see the new Alfred Hitchcock movie, *North by Northwest*, at the Wiltern. He loved Alfred Hitchcock movies and he couldn't wait to see this latest. He arrived at the theater a half-hour early, as usual, and was first in line, as usual. He had his turkey sandwich with him, as usual, and he was first inside the theater and first in his seat, as usual. The theater filled up pretty quickly and it was not a bad crowd for a Wednesday at 12:30 in the afternoon. There were the usual cartoons and coming attractions. Then suddenly the M-G-M lion was roaring—Benjamin liked the M-G-M lion, but this M-G-M lion was different— it wasn't in black-and-white or full color as he'd seen it a hundred times before; no this M-G-M lion was green, the entire background color was green. That, along with the pulse-pounding music, made Benjamin know he was in for something special. Then the credits came on—the names moving on and off the screen against vertical lines. All the Alfred Hitchcock movies Benjamin had ever seen had been Paramount films in VistaVision, so it was weird to have this one be from M-G-M. It was still in VistaVision, according to the credits, so Benjamin was happy. The vertical lines turned into what looked like the side of an office building and you could see the traffic and streets reflected in the windows (almost like a mirror). The music was by Benjamin's favorite, Bernard Herrmann (every time Benjamin loved the music in a movie, it ended up being by Bernard Herrmann), and it was so exciting that Benjamin's leg was shaking in rhythm to it.

He loved every single second of *North by Northwest* and it instantly replaced *The Seventh Voyage of Sinbad* as the greatest motion picture ever made. As was his wont, Benjamin sat through the second feature so he could see *North by Northwest* again, and it was even better the second time through. He couldn't make up his mind which was his favorite scene: Lester Townsend of Unipo being stabbed in the back at the United Nations, the drunken car ride, the auction, the crop-dusting scene where Cary Grant was chased by the airplane, or the ending chase all over Mount Rushmore.

On the way back to the Erro, Benjamin hummed the music aloud as he walked south on Western, pretending he was being chased by a crop-dusting airplane.

That became Benjamin's new fun and exciting thing— humming the music to *North by Northwest*, while pretending he was being chased by a crop-dusting airplane. He did this wherever he went, whether to the market, on his way to the Helms truck to get a chocolate donut, to the miniature golf course, or even in the back yard. He went over to Index Radio and Records to see if there was a record of the music, but it wasn't in the big catalog they kept on the front counter. He saw the movie five more times at the Wiltern.

When it wasn't playing there anymore, he began to follow the movie to whatever theater it was playing in. He saw it at the Picwood, he saw it at the El Rey (where it was playing with *The Five Pennies*), and when it finally showed up at the Stadium, he saw it there. One gray day, Benjamin even took a bus to Hollywood to see *North by Northwest* at the New View, a small theater on Hollywood Boulevard, where he loved it all over again.

When he came out of the theater that afternoon, it was pouring rain, even though it was the dog days of summer. Benjamin didn't have an umbrella with him, but he didn't care because he loved being in the rain without an umbrella, loved feeling the rain pour down on him. He ran down Hollywood Boulevard pretending he was being chased by a crop-dusting airplane, getting soaked in the process. Was there anything better than running down Hollywood Boulevard in the pouring rain pretending you were being chased by a crop-dusting airplane and getting soaked in the process? Not likely, in Benjamin's rambunctious opinion.

He ran over to Wilcox where the bus stop was. He looked up at the clock near the Warner Cinerama and saw that it was three-thirty. He could see the stores and restaurants on the boulevard reflected in the rainy streets, and he thought that was a truly magical sight. He wanted to go into Coffee Dan's and have a Dodger burger, but he needed to get home before dinner time. There was no bus in sight, so instead of just standing in the rain and waiting, he ran down towards Highland, where there was another bus stop.

As he ran with the rain slapping down on him, Benjamin looked in the store windows he passed and at the movie theaters that lined both sides of the street. At Las Palmas he had to stop and catch his breath—he was drenched, sopping wet through and through. He was in front of a store called Pickwick Books, so he stepped inside to get out of the rain for a minute. He stood there, dripping on the floor, and could not believe his eyes. There were books everywhere, miles and miles of books, more books than he'd ever seen in a store. He'd have to come back to Pickwick and spend an hour or two when he wasn't dripping wet and didn't have to get home for dinner, because he loved being around books, looking at the covers and reading bits and pieces from all the ones that interested him.

Benjamin came out of Pickwick, ran one more block to Highland and got there just as his bus was pulling up. It was a wonderful bus ride home, seeing all the different streets with the rain coming down, people scurrying about with their umbrellas, colors blurring crazily on the rain-soaked pavement, as if someone had washed the street with hundreds of watercolors.

* * *

Benjamin's leg-shaking had reached epic proportions because his apprehension about starting junior high school had reached epic proportions. The beginning of school was only a week away and he was feeling panic in every bone of his body. He and Minnie had gone shopping for new school supplies—that part was fine. He'd gotten a new three-ring notebook, a new plastic pen and pencil holder for the notebook (with lots of nice brand new pens and pencils to put in it), lots of lined paper for the notebook, a ruler, a pencil sharpener, a nice pink eraser and various other school necessities. Yes, that part was fine and he liked all his new school supplies very much indeed. It was the clothing part that was not fine, it was the buying of the gym shorts and the dreaded jockstrap that was not fine. He hated the dopey-looking gym shorts and he was totally repulsed by the ugly drab-colored jockstrap. What was wrong with wearing plain old underpants under the gym shorts? Jeffrey had said that they made you wear the jockstrap for support. Benjamin didn't see how the jockstrap gave any more support than his very own underpants.

He went into his closet and tried on the jockstrap and looked in the mirror. The front part was quite ugly-looking, but at least resembled underpants, albeit ridged and heavier. The real problem was the back of the jockstrap—or, more to the point, the fact that there was no back to the jockstrap. Benjamin turned and looked and there was his very own rear end on view, like the food at Ontra Cafeteria. The gym shorts were equally as bad—no matter which way he wore them, they always looked like they were on backwards.

Benjamin had a nauseous feeling in his stomach that would not go away, and his poor leg had taken on a life of its own. As if that weren't bad enough, Benjamin had just seen yet another movie at the Picfair Theater, *Horrors of the Black Museum*, and that movie was just about the most frightening thing Benjamin had ever witnessed, and that was based solely on the first scene—a scene in which a pretty lady received a lovely gift—a lovely pair of binoculars. And when the pretty lady had put those lovely binoculars up to her lovely eyes there was a loud click and suddenly she screamed sickeningly; the lovely binoculars fell to the floor revealing two bloodstained knives sticking out from the lenses, which had apparently found their way into the lovely woman's formerly-lovely eyeballs. Well, that scene, which occurred within the first five minutes of the film, sent Benjamin Kritzer scurrying up the aisle never to return to the theater auditorium, except for occasionally peeking in the door.

Yes, Benjamin felt his life was beginning to resemble a horror movie, The Curse of Benjamin Kritzer, with new terrors and new horrors waiting around every corner. His whole world was turning upside-down and he was continuously ill-at-ease.

The day before he was to start his new school, Benjamin was a total wreck. Earlier that day he'd done a test walk to see which route he liked better: walking down Airdrome and entering through the back of the school, or walking down 18th and entering through the front of the school. He'd gotten a letter from the school, telling him which classroom to report to—something called Homeroom. He settled on the Airdrome route because it was more familiar to him and because he passed by Crescent Heights Elementary School and he felt that would give him comfort somehow.

That night he could barely eat his dinner (it didn't help that Minnie had made liver and onions, Benjamin's least favorite food on earth—what *was* she thinking?), and he was

93

too antsy to even watch *The Ed Sullivan Show.* He took a long hot shower in his parents' bathroom and then he went into his room and organized his notebook.

Bedtime came, and he said goodnight to everyone. Minnie had already laid out his clothes for his first day at junior high school. In fact, everything was ready except for Benjamin. He thought about running away, thought about escaping to Kritzerland and never coming back. It was hopeless, however, and he knew it. Tomorrow he'd be starting junior high school and there was nothing he could do about it. Minnie came in to say goodnight and tuck Benjamin in. She said, "Well, get a good night's sleep because you have to get up very early. You know, Benjamin, the early bird catches the worm." And with that, she shut off the light and closed the door.

Benjamin stared up at the ceiling and thought about the early bird catching the worm. He wondered if there was a late bird and if the late bird ever caught the worm. He wondered if the worm ever caught the early bird. He reached up to the table and got his transistor radio. He put the earpiece in his ear, turned the radio on and twirled the dial, trying to find a song he liked. He stopped when he heard The Fleetwoods singing *Put Your Head on My Shoulder.*

Put your head on my shoulder
Hold me in your arms, baby

He thought how much easier it would be if only Susan were here, starting junior high school with him. Then he wouldn't be frightened at all, because how could you be frightened if Susan Pomeroy was holding your hand and walking with you to a new school?

Put your head on my shoulder
Whisper in my ear, baby

But Susan wasn't there to put her head on Benjamin's shoulder; he was on his own and he was somehow going to have to get through this by himself. After a while he fell asleep. He dreamed, and in his dream he was being chased across the junior high school campus, chased by everyone in the school. He was dressed only in his jockstrap, and he ran and ran but he wasn't running fast, he couldn't work up any speed at all, and they were catching up to him. He ran, *trying* to go faster, and then quite suddenly his feet left the ground and he was airborne. He was going up, up, up into the sky, flying, soaring above all the people who were chasing him. The last thing he remembered thinking was, "They'll never catch me now."

He awoke the next morning, dressed, ate breakfast, took a deep breath, and went off to his new world.

CHAPTER EIGHT

Junior High School

As soon as he walked through the back gate of Louis Pasteur Junior High School, Benjamin Kritzer knew he was in trouble. It was a madhouse. It was absolute chaos. He found himself adrift in a sea of kids—walking, running, pushing, shoving, laughing, screaming kids. Kids of every shape, size and color. Benjamin didn't know if he was coming or going, although if he'd been given a choice he would have preferred going.

It took him fifteen minutes to find his Homeroom (Room 107) and he only found it because some kind adult had finally pointed him in the right direction. He got there in the nick of time and got seated just before the bell rang. The Homeroom teacher, Mrs. Rose, a dour middle-aged lady in a pale blue dress, her hair done up in a bun, called roll, and as each new student raised their hand and said "present" (she'd told everyone that they had to raise their hand and say "present"), she handed them their class schedule and locker assignment and combination.

"Now, class," Mrs. Rose said dourly, "you are going to begin every day with Homeroom. Here you will find out about events such as assemblies and changes in schedule and so forth and so on. Going to junior high school is going to be very different than elementary school. Now, look at the schedules that I have passed out to you."

There was a mass rustling of paper as the class looked at their schedules.

"Now, each class is called a period and there are eight periods per day," Mrs. Rose continued. "You have eight minutes between periods in which to get to your next class. This is called the passing period. Now, if you are late to your next class, you will receive a tardy mark, and so forth and so on."

As she continued chattering away, Benjamin's head felt like it was going to explode. Periods, passing periods, lockers, tardy marks—this was already more horrifying than The Curse of Benjamin Kritzer. This was Attack of the Junior High School. He looked at his class schedule— History, Math, English, Wood Shop, Gym, Science, and Agriculture—and wondered why each class had to be a period. Couldn't some classes be a comma or a semi-colon? But no, everything at Louis Pasteur Junior High School was a period, even lunch was a period—apparently that was the only form of punctuation they knew about. Benjamin knew about the various forms of punctuation because he'd learned about them in one classroom with one teacher at Crescent Heights Elementary School, where he wished he was right this very minute.

Mrs. Rose was still talking. It was becoming obvious that that was what Mrs. Rose did—talk. It seemed as though she hadn't taken a breath since Homeroom had started.

"Now," she dourly went on, "every morning at 9:52 precisely, Dr. Rogers, our school principal, will speak over the public address system. Now, when Dr. Rogers speaks over the public address system, you must stop and listen very carefully because Dr. Rogers makes important announcements and you must take note of them and so forth and so on."

Benjamin sat there, wondering why Mrs. Rose began so many sentences with the word "now" and why she kept saying "and so forth and so on" over and over again. Finally, the bell rang and put an end to Mrs. Rose's endless monologue, and Benjamin and the other students got up and headed off to their first-period class.

Benjamin's first-period class was History and he got to the classroom within the eight-minute passing period thereby avoiding the dreaded tardy mark. His teacher, Mr. Sitton, was a disheveled-looking man with a wrinkled shirt and wrinkled pants (he looked like a bag of laundry, Benjamin thought), who always seemed like he was talking *over* the students' heads. Not much happened in History class other than Mr. Sitton passing out a thick textbook to everyone.

On his way to his second class, Agriculture, the public address system crackled and came to life and the voice of Dr. Rogers came on. Dr. Rogers, Benjamin realized immediately, was a woman, and a cantankerous-sounding one at that.

"Good morning, students, I am Dr. Rogers and I welcome you to the first day of the new semester. We hope you will have a rewarding experience here at Louis Pasteur Junior High School, but you must be on your best behavior. We do not tolerate misbehavior at this school. We deal with misbehavior with swift justice. We are watching you for any kind of misbehavior."

Benjamin noticed that everyone had stopped to listen to Dr. Rogers. It reminded him of that movie he'd just seen on Channel 9—*1984*, where everyone had to stop and listen to the voice on the public address system, because if you didn't stop to listen to the voice on the public address system then the Thought Police would come and take you away because Big Brother was watching you and would not tolerate people who didn't stop and listen to the voice on the public address system. Benjamin wondered if Louis Pasteur Junior High School was going to be like *1984*, only instead of Big Brother watching you, it would be Dr. Rogers watching you, watching you for any kind of misbehavior. It was all very strange, but it was over soon enough and afterwards Benjamin had to run all the way to Agriculture because Dr. Rogers had used up two of his eight passing-period minutes.

In Agriculture, Benjamin and the other students were told that they'd be planting vegetables and watching them grow, all throughout the semester. Planting vegetables seemed like a fine idea to Benjamin; at least it was much better than having to actually eat them. Benjamin thought that his Agriculture teacher, Mr. Bodine, *looked* like a vegetable—short and squat and red-faced, like a radish.

After Agriculture there was a ten-minute recess. Recess, unlike Lunch, wasn't a period, so Benjamin called recess a hyphen. So far, recess was the only thing Benjamin liked about Louis Pasteur Junior High School and that was because they had something called Hash Lines where you could get hot chocolate and sugar cookies and other snacks. Benjamin bought a sugar cookie and hot chocolate. The sugar cookie was incredibly delicious, maybe the best cookie he'd ever had. It was fairly big, still warm, and chewy, and it went very well with the equally delicious hot chocolate. Both cookie and hot chocolate smelled wonderful, too, and Benjamin knew that he'd have to have a sugar cookie and hot chocolate every single day.

Before recess was over, Benjamin found his locker and put his History textbook into it, so he didn't have to lug it around with him. His next period was Gym class. This was the class he was most terrified of. He nervously followed the other students into the gym building, where they were told to go into the locker room and change into their gym clothes. The locker room was very large and filled with lockers which, Benjamin supposed, was only normal for something called a locker room. The noise level was painful, with overlapping voices reverberating off the walls crazily. Benjamin found a locker as far away from everyone else as possible, opened it and stood behind the locker door so that he could have a modicum of privacy. He then undressed as quickly as he could, put on the disgusting jockstrap and baggy gym shorts and plain t-shirt as quickly as he could and left the locker room as quickly as he could.

Outside, on the gym field, the gym teacher, a tough-looking, no-nonsense man named Mr. Mark, had everyone form three lines, one in back of the other. Benjamin managed to get in the third line, as far away from Mr. Mark's sight as possible. Mr. Mark then performed what he called a jockstrap check, where each boy had to show him that he was indeed wearing a jockstrap. Benjamin wondered what would happen if Mr. Mark discovered someone was wearing underpants instead of a jockstrap. Would that unfortunate person receive a bad mark from Mr. Mark?

Then Mr. Mark made everyone do jumping jacks. He demonstrated how to properly do them, and then counted loudly as the class began to do twenty-five of them. Benjamin tried, oh, yes, he tried, but no matter how hard he tried he couldn't get the hang of the jumping jacks. Everyone else in the class seemed to be doing their jumping jacks just fine, but Benjamin couldn't get the coordination between his feet going out and in and his hands going up and down and he looked like some out-of-control window-wiper. Mr. Mark was walking up and down the lines and when he got to Benjamin he just stared at him, as if Benjamin were some form of dead plant life. Benjamin smiled wanly at him, and Mr. Mark gave him a withering look and moved on.

Next, the class was instructed to do ten pushups. Mr. Mark demonstrated the way he liked to have pushups done, and then he told the class to hit the ground and begin doing their pushups. Benjamin did three pushups and could do no more. He tried, but his arms would not raise his body no matter how much he willed them to do so. Some of the other kids made it to ten, but at least Benjamin was not alone in not being able to finish them. Then they did some insane exercise called the six-count burpee, which consisted of bending down, kicking your legs backwards then back to where they were, and then getting up again, all the while thrusting your arms out like Commando Cody did when he was about to fly.

Then Mr. Mark instructed everyone to do a lap. Benjamin didn't know what doing a lap meant, but apparently all the other kids did, so he just followed them. It was almost as if the rest of the class had attended a rehearsal for Gym class that Benjamin had somehow missed. In any case, a lap was running around a dirt track one time. Benjamin ran at a medium pace and as he ran he did take notice of the girls' gym field where there were girls in baggy green gym shorts also doing exercise. He thought the girls looked much nicer in their baggy shorts than the boys did, and he wondered if they, too, had to wear a jockstrap. As Benjamin ran, a tall, muscular boy bumped into him, almost knocking him over. The boy turned to him with a malevolent look in his eyes and said, "Get out of my way, jerk. And stay out of my way." The boy ran on. Benjamin hadn't realized he was in anyone's way and he thought that he'd be more than happy to stay out of that boy's way forever.

At the end of the lap, Mr. Mark told everyone to hit the showers. Apparently expressions with "hit" in them were Mr. Mark's favorites—"hit the ground", "hit the showers", hit this, hit that. Benjamin and the rest of the boys went back into the locker room. Benjamin took off his gym clothes and put them in his locker. He waited until most of the other boys had gone off to the showers and then he made his way toward them. The showers were filled with naked boys, all chattering away madly. Benjamin was mortified. He hated standing naked in front of anyone, let alone a bunch of strangers. He found a shower toward the back and let the water run over him. The water was tepid.

If there was anything that Benjamin Kritzer hated it was tepid water. He liked hot water, really hot water, but the water people at Louis Pasteur Junior High School apparently didn't care about what Benjamin Kritzer liked or wanted, and so he had to endure the tepid lukewarm water. He stood there, tepid water and all, until most of the others had gone, and then Benjamin left the shower room, too.

On the way out, he passed a large window with what looked like a fence on the front of it, where towels were being thrown at the wet boys coming out of the shower. Benjamin managed to catch one—it was warm and had a pungent smell, something like toasted coconut. The towels were white with weird ridges. Benjamin immediately wrapped his around his waist and hurried to his locker. He dried off and got dressed as fast as he could and got out of that locker room as if he were the Road Runner.

Thankfully, his next period, fourth period, was lunch, so he had fifty minutes to recover from the horror that had been Gym class. He found a bench where he could sit alone and opened his lunch bag. Minnie had made him a meatloaf sandwich on white bread, and there were also some potato chips and an apple. He looked around the lunch court and did not see one familiar face from Crescent Heights. What he did see was a lot of people in groups. Everyone had friends or seemed to know each other. He nibbled at his meatloaf sandwich, took a bite of the apple and threw the rest of his lunch in the trashcan. He went to the boys' room, and went to the bathroom. When he was finished he looked in the mirror. His hair was ridiculous— he'd forgotten to bring a comb to Gym class and his hair had dried every which way hair could possibly dry, in every direction, going this way and that way, and Benjamin felt he looked like someone from that movie about crazy people, *The Snake Pit*, which he'd also recently seen on Channel 9.

The bell rang and Benjamin looked at his schedule. His next period was Science in Bungalow Three. The only problem was that Benjamin had no idea where Bungalow Three was. He saw a group of buildings to his left, so he walked over there—unfortunately, those Bungalows were Seven and Eight. He crossed the yard, knowing that his passing-period minutes were ticking away, and he found another Bungalow. Unfortunately, this Bungalow was Bungalow One. He walked further and found Bungalows Four and Five. Then he found Bungalow Two. Why they didn't provide maps with the class schedules was beyond him. Benjamin saw a student walking and he went up to him and asked if he knew where Bungalow Three was. The student, a boy who resembled King Kong, looked at Benjamin and said, "Find it yourself," and continued walking. As Benjamin continued his quest to find Bungalow Three, he was beginning to wonder if there were any friendly people at this school.

He finally found it. It was tucked back behind Bungalow Two, totally hidden from view, and he made it there just as the bell was ringing. He sat next to a rather large boy who smelled quite bad. Despite the bad smell, Benjamin smiled at him. "What are you looking at?" the large smelly boy said in a nasal voice. Benjamin wanted to say, "I'm looking at a large smelly boy, that's what I'm looking at," but he thought better of it and merely turned away. Not much else happened in Science class, although he did get another thick textbook.

In Math he received another thick textbook, and in English yet another, and he deposited Science, Math and

English textbooks into his locker, which was now beginning to resemble a library. He went off to Wood Shop, where he discovered he had the teacher Jeffrey had warned him about—the eraser-throwing Mr. Godowsky.

There were no desks or chairs in Wood Shop. There were work benches and band saws and regular saws and wood—lots and lots of wood. The class stood in the center of the large building while Mr. Godowsky called out everyone's name. As each person answered "here" or "present," Mr. Godowsky would cast his beady eyes on them, and look at them with a scowl on his pock-marked face. As Mr. Godowsky began explaining what would be happening in Wood Shop, Benjamin looked around at the variety of saws and different machines. Benjamin had used a saw before, because Ernie had one in the garage. Benjamin had sawed through a box of Grape Nuts cereal which, at the time, he'd found highly amusing.

"You!" Benjamin heard a voice say.

He turned around just in time to see an eraser sailing by his head, only narrowly missing him. The crew-cut Mr. Godowsky was glaring at him. "Next time I won't miss, sonny. What's your name?"

"Benjamin Kritzer."

"Well, look at me when I'm talking and pay attention! You're not going to cause me trouble, are you? You look like trouble to me, Kritzer. I've got my eye on you."

Benjamin didn't really want Mr. Godowsky's eye on him, but he'd been daydreaming and had raised the wrath of Mr. Godowsky and now Mr. Godowsky had his eye on him. For the rest of the class, Benjamin paid attention and never took his eyes off Mr. Godowsky who, in turn, never took his eyes off Benjamin.

The three o'clock bell finally rang and Benjamin's first day in junior high school was thankfully over. He felt as if he'd been body-slammed repeatedly, like one of the wrestlers that Jeffrey watched on Channel 5. He was sore (his three pushups had really made his arms and upper chest hurt) and he was tired. Luckily, no homework had been assigned, so he left all his thick textbooks in his locker and only took his notebook home with him. He walked west along Airdrome and, as he passed Crescent Heights, he ran his hand along the fence, wishing he could be back in the uncomplicated world of his elementary school rather than this strange new world he was now in.

CHAPTER NINE

Turning Twelve, and The End of the 50s

As the weeks went by, school began to get easier for Benjamin. He got used to where his classes were, and he was now able to get to them without fear of being tardy (even with Dr. Rogers' two-minute daily interruptions). At least certain classes, like English and Agriculture, were bearable, while others, like Gym and Wood Shop, were not.

Benjamin had begun to eat in the cafeteria for lunch. He didn't really like the food, but he did like the *names* of the food—Spring Garden Special, Shepherd's Pie, Chicken ala King and Friday Surprise. He also was fond of the little dishes of Jell-O squares, which he liked to pick up and bounce on his cafeteria tray. He always sat by himself, because even though he finally had seen some faces he knew from Crescent Heights, he had never really been friendly with any of those people. It wasn't that he didn't want a friend; he actually thought it would be nice to have a friend, an ally, but no one even made an attempt to talk to him, and he was too shy to start conversations with people he didn't know and who certainly didn't give the appearance of wanting to be friendly.

In Agriculture, they'd already planted some carrots and radishes, but nothing had begun to grow yet. Mr. Bodine had also let them pick out some flowers to plant—from little packets of seeds. Benjamin liked those little packets of seeds because of the colorful pictures on the front of them. Benjamin had picked out Snapdragons because he always liked the houses he passed that had them growing in front.

Gym class continued to be the bane of Benjamin's existence. Quite simply, not only were the dressing and undressing and showering and jockstrap horrifying, but he hated any kind of sports and that's all they did in Gym class. They'd already played basketball and volleyball and football. Benjamin would always be the last one chosen for a team and he would always be placed where he could do the least harm.

He simply didn't understand the attraction of dribbling a ball and shooting it into a basket. Nor did he understand the attraction of hitting a ball over a net, or the attraction of getting a touchdown while being chased by a bunch of crazed people intent on knocking you to the ground with as much force as humanly possible. He would much rather have just watched the girls' Gym class—*that* he understood the attraction of just fine. Plus, that boy who'd bumped into him that first day (his name was Butch Polsky—wasn't that just perfect) had continued to give Benjamin a hard time, always purposely bumping into him and calling him names. Not to mention the Black twins, Ronald and Donald Earl, who loved to snap towels at the behinds of unsuspecting boys (like Benjamin) coming out of the shower.

Benjamin also hated homework, and tried to do as little of it as he could. After all, wasn't having to sit in school from eight in the morning until three in the afternoon enough punishment for one individual? Why did they have to give homework on top of that? Whose brilliant idea was homework anyway? Benjamin came up with a spelled-backwards word to describe the person who invented homework. It had come to him one night while he was buttering his bread with a knife: efink. Yes, efink, that was a perfect name for the person who invented homework.

In History, they'd begun to learn about the Bill of Rights. Benjamin was amused by the name "Bill of Rights". He thought if there was a "Bill of Rights", then surely there must be a "Henry of Lefts". There was a girl in History class, Glenda Allen, who Benjamin thought was very pretty and he would always smile at her whenever he got bored of hearing about the Bill of Rights or looking at Mr. Sitton's nasty wrinkled shirts with the green stains under the armpits.

One day, on the way out of the classroom, Glenda handed Benjamin a piece of folded-up notebook paper. As he walked to his next class, he excitedly opened it, wondering what she might have written him. On the lined notebook paper, Glenda had written: Why are you smiling at me all the time? Stop it. Glenda.

Benjamin and Math were a fairly hopeless combination. He was good at adding and subtracting, however anything beyond that was simply an annoyance. But at least he was settling into his junior high school routine, and even though he didn't have any friends, he was managing to get through the days without too much trouble.

*   *   *

Benjamin got to miss school (hooray) for Rosh Hashanah, and the Kritzers went to the temple on Main Street with Grandma and Grandpa Gelfinbaum. After temple, Benjamin went to POP, went on the Flight to Mars ride, played some Skeeball in the Penny Arcade, and then visited Mr. Szymond in the magic shop. Benjamin had been saving up so he could purchase the trick knife Mr. Szymond had shown him the last time he'd been there—the knife with the retractable blade. When you pressed that blade to your stomach, it would disappear into the haft of the knife, giving the impression that the knife had gone into your stomach, when, of course, it really hadn't. That was just irresistible to Benjamin, and luckily he had just enough money to buy it.

At Rosh Hashanah dinner that night, Benjamin waited for Jeffrey to say something mean (this was inevitable), and when he finally did, Benjamin, in front of everyone, pulled out the knife and said, "I've had it with you" and lunged at Jeffrey, stabbing him in the stomach. Aunt Lena screamed, Minnie's mouth was open so big she could have put a trout in it and Jeffrey just stood there, curiously looking at the knife, which Benjamin then withdrew. As soon as she saw it wasn't real, Aunt Lena breathed a sigh of relief and said, "Oh, it's just one of his tricks. What a bad boy."

Jeffrey lunged at Benjamin and said, "Give me that" but Benjamin was too fast for him and got behind Ernie before

Jeffrey could get to him. Minnie started yelling, "Benjamin, what is the matter with you? What did I do to deserve such a child?" At that point, Grandpa Gelfinbaum came out of the bathroom, looked at everyone and said, "I made a stool." There was really no comeback to that line, so everyone sat down at the table and had crumb cake.

*   *   *

On Friday, October 2nd, Benjamin was sitting in the den, watching television by himself. Minnie and Ernie had gone out to play cards, and Jeffrey was out with his club friends, presumably getting drunk on Ripple (Jeffrey had already regaled Benjamin with his tales of vomiting up endless amounts of Ripple). He'd gone to the new Italian restaurant that had opened next to the miniature golf course, Scarantino's (the Kritzers had already eaten there several times and liked it very much) and gotten his favorite, spaghetti and meatballs, to take home. He loved getting food to go and eating it while he watched television—that was just the best. Benjamin didn't have any favorite television shows on Friday nights, but he didn't mind *Rawhide* and *77 Sunset Strip*, so he watched those while he ate his spaghetti and meatballs.

At ten o'clock he went to the television and switched channels, stopping to see what was on Channel 2. There was a new show premiering, and Benjamin was intrigued by the title, *The Twilight Zone*, so he went back to the couch to watch. As soon as he heard the opening music he was hooked—it was weird and moody. The episode was called *Where Is Everybody?* and by the time it was over Benjamin had already decided that *The Twilight Zone* was the finest television program he'd ever seen. It was creepy and strange and the story had an excellent twist at the end and the whole thing just gave Benjamin the willies. He watched the credits after it was over and was amazed to see that the music was by his favorite, Bernard Herrmann. He decided right then and there that he would never miss an episode of *The Twilight Zone*—it would become his Friday night ritual from that moment on.

And so it was—every Friday night from then on Benjamin would go to Scarantino's, get his spaghetti and meatballs to go, and come home and wait for *The Twilight Zone* to come on Channel 2 at ten o'clock. It seemed like every episode was better than the one before. Towards the end of October, they aired an episode that became Benjamin's favorite so far. It was called *Walking Distance*, and was about an unhappy man who somehow finds himself walking in his old neighborhood—only the neighborhood is as it was when he was a kid. He sees his parents, who don't know who he is (that *really* gave Benjamin the willies) and he even sees and talks to himself as a child. The whole episode really got to Benjamin and he replayed it in his mind, over and over again.

* * *

Benjamin was beginning to realize how much he didn't like most of his classes. He simply didn't care about History or Science or Math or Wood Shop and, of course, he absolutely loathed Gym class. He liked recess and lunch, those were just fine, but his daily visits to Homeroom had become really annoying (Mrs. Rose literally never stopped talking from the minute Homeroom began to the bell twenty minutes later). He also didn't like having to stand for two minutes every day listening to the rather inane pronouncements of the principal, Dr. Rogers, but she was the principal, Benjamin supposed, so she could do what she wanted. It didn't help that Benjamin had finally gotten a look at Dr. Rogers at an assembly, and she was one of the most unappetizing-looking people he'd ever seen—short, squat, with an ugly mole on her cheek and with a head that was way too big for her body. In fact, Benjamin thought she'd fit right in on *The Twilight Zone.*

* * *

In late November, a movie called *Ben-Hur* opened at the Egyptian Theater in Hollywood. Benjamin really wanted to see *Ben-Hur* because it was in 65mm and stereophonic sound and because he'd read that it had a chariot race. He began to pester Minnie, but she wasn't having any of it.

"Why can't we go?" Benjamin would ask.

"Benjamin, stop nagging me. It's reserved seats and it's a big pain in the rear end," Minnie would reply.

"But *why* can't we go?" Benjamin would ask again, hoping the repetition would annoy his mother enough that she would simply say "yes" to get him to shut up. Unfortunately, that ploy wasn't working.

"Benjamin, you can ask until the cows come home, but I'm not schlepping up to Hollywood."

Benjamin slowly turned to his mother. "I can ask until the cows come home? I didn't even know the cows were away? I didn't even know we had cows."

"Benjamin, you are really getting on my nerves. Why don't you go play in traffic?"

"Should I play in traffic until the cows come home?"

Minnie turned to him, shaking the ladle in her hand. "Stop with the cows already. You are giving me a migraine. We're not seeing *Ben-Hur* and that's that. If that doesn't make you happy, tell it to the Indians."

Benjamin wondered if he should tell it to the Indians before or after the cows came home, but he didn't say it aloud because he did, after all, want to see *Ben-Hur* and he knew if he kept nagging that eventually she would buckle under and take him.

* * *

The beginning of December brought rain, a great big king-sized package of rain. It poured every day and night for almost a week which, of course, Benjamin loved.

For Benjamin's twelfth birthday, Ernie took the entire family to Kelbo's on Pico, near Sawtelle. Kelbo's was one of Benjamin's favorites, and he always had the same thing there: salad with their unique and absolutely delicious Thousand Island dressing, a barbecued beef sandwich with Kelbo's special sauce, and two spare ribs. The only thing left on Benjamin's plate after a meal at Kelbo's were two spare ribs with nothing left on them.

After dinner, Ernie dropped Benjamin at the Four Star Theater on Wilshire so he could see *The Angry Red Planet*, which was his choice for a birthday movie. *The Angry Red Planet* was yet another movie about Mars and Martian monsters, so of course Benjamin had to see it. It was also in a new process called Cinemagic, which basically made everything on Mars look orange and brown. Not really so magical, but Benjamin liked to keep up with all the new movie processes.

When the movie let out, Ernie was waiting there to pick him up. Benjamin still hadn't been given his birthday present, and all the way home he wondered if he was actually going to get one. So, imagine his surprise when he went into his bedroom and found a brand new small television set. He couldn't believe it—his very own television set (well, not quite—he did have to let Jeffrey watch it, too). Now there would be no arguing with his parents over what show would be watched—from now on he could watch whatever he wanted whenever he wanted.

* * *

The rain continued to fall. The streets were completely flooded and Benjamin sometimes found the water almost up past his ankle when he'd inadvertently step in a puddle on the way to school. His weekly routine of watching *The Twilight Zone* and eating spaghetti and meatballs from Scarantino's continued, only now he got to watch in his very own room, sitting all alone in the dark, which made it ever so much more creepy and weird.

In Agriculture class, Benjamin's vegetables had begun to grow, and he actually picked one of the radishes and brought it home, and each and every Kritzer dutifully tried a bite of Benjamin's Very Own Radish. Everyone seemed to think it tasted like a radish, and everyone said it was very good except Jeffrey, who spit his bite out on the kitchen floor.

* * *

Christmas vacation finally arrived on December 18th. School let out at noon, and Benjamin was entirely thrilled that he would not have to return to Louis Pasteur Junior High School for two weeks. Best of all, *Li'l Abner*, the movie he'd seen being filmed, had just opened at the Wiltern Theater. Ernie had promised him he could see it after school on Friday, so he was waiting for Benjamin at the back gate. He drove him straight to the Wiltern and let him off at twelve-twenty, just in time for the twelve-thirty show (Ernie had had Al make Benjamin his usual turkey sandwich).

Benjamin quickly sat down in his tenth-row aisle seat and took out his turkey sandwich. There were the usual coming attractions, cartoon and newsreel. Then, the Paramount mountain was on the screen in all its Technicolor glory, followed by Benjamin's favorite, the VistaVision logo. The credits came on, and Benjamin immediately recognized the Dogpatch set he'd seen when he and Minnie had watched the movie being shot on the Paramount lot.

The people began to sing a song about a typical day in Dogpatch USA. Benjamin instantly fell in love with *Li'l Abner*. During the song, characters were introduced, characters with names like Earthquake McGoon and Moonbeam McSwine and Marryin' Sam, and it was all too wonderful for words. The costumes were funny and colorful and the whole thing resembled a cartoon and Benjamin wanted to move to Dogpatch right then and there.

Suddenly, there was the incandescently beautiful woman he'd met that day on the soundstage, Leslie Parrish, in her skimpy Daisy Mae outfit. She was even more beautiful and breathtaking on the big Wiltern screen than she'd been in person. Benjamin remembered the sweet smell of her when she'd leaned down and kissed him on the cheek and he was smitten with her all over again.

The scene they'd watched being shot for hours and hours, with the pretty woman saying, "But *Bullsie*," lasted for all of thirty seconds in the actual movie. Benjamin sat through the second feature, and then stayed for another showing of *Li'l Abner*. He went back to the Wiltern three more times during the week to see it again.

*   *   *

Christmas came and with it came a brand new Cadillac. Minnie had wanted a brand new Cadillac for quite some time and had been quite vocal about it because all her friends had Cadillacs and she just couldn't stand having to drive an Oldsmobile one minute longer. Ernie had surprised her with it on Christmas morning, and Minnie had gone into paroxysms of joy, fawning over it as if it was the most valuable treasure in all the world. The whole family had to get into the Cadillac (while still in their pajamas—Ernie, thankfully, had the decency to put on pants) and drive around the neighborhood, parading the gorgeously painted light-blue car for all to see.

Minnie gave Ernie several things, including a spiffy new Remington Electric Shaver. Jeffrey got some clothes (Jeffrey was becoming very clothes conscious—apparently that was something one did in high school), some money, and a big jar of pink pomade for his hair (Benjamin thought it smelled like bubble gum). Benjamin, whose new television was really supposed to be a combination birthday and Christmas present, still got some nice things from various relatives and friends, and Minnie and Ernie did give him a few presents anyway, including a subscription to *TV Guide* so he wouldn't have to spend the fifteen cents every week.

* * *

Over the days between Christmas and New Year's, Benjamin sat in his room and watched all his favorite television shows—*Wanted: Dead or Alive, Mr. Lucky, The Jack Benny Show*—as well as various end-of-the-year specials. There were a lot of end-of-the-year specials because this particular end-of-the-year *was* special—it was not only the end of a year, it was the end of a decade. Benjamin couldn't get over it; in just a few short days the 1950s would be a thing of the past. After December 31st, it would be the 1960s, and Benjamin, who didn't like change, was quite nervous about it.

Still and all, he'd managed to adjust to junior high school much more quickly than he could have ever imagined, so maybe he'd adjust to the 1960s quickly, too. At least he had high hopes about adjusting to the 1960s quickly, because the night before New Year's Eve, he'd watched Perry Como on television. Perry had sung a song from a movie Benjamin had seen and liked—*A Hole in the Head*. The song was called *High Hopes* and Benjamin thought it was a perfect expression of how he felt about whatever the future might hold. He could overcome anything, that's what he felt, even the most difficult obstacles (well, except for Math and Science and Wood Shop and Gym—those were and would always be beyond him) because, after all, wasn't he the unique and special Benjamin Kritzer?

The next day, December 31st, the last day Benjamin or anyone else would ever spend in the 1950s, he ran over to Index Radio and Records and bought the 45 of *High Hopes*. They didn't have one with Perry Como, though, so he got the one with Frank Sinatra who, Minnie informed Benjamin when he'd told her they didn't have a Perry Como version, was not exactly chopped liver. Who exactly *was* chopped liver was another question, and besides, just how could a person be chopped liver anyway? But to Minnie Kritzer and the saying people, all things were possible.

Minnie and Ernie were going to a big New Year's Eve bash that night, and Jeffrey was going to some party with his friends. Minnie had told Benjamin he could come along to their party, but Benjamin didn't really want to be around a bunch of people he didn't know. He just wanted to stay home and watch television and listen to records.

While Minnie got ready for the party (that was a several-hours ordeal), Ernie drove Benjamin to Piece o' Pizza (Benjamin was crazy about their pizza, and he liked the sign in front of the restaurant—"Had a piece lately?") so Benjamin could get a small pizza pie and a salad to go. By the time they got home, Jeffrey was just leaving. He was wearing a new sweater, khaki pants, and his hair was filled with that bubble gum-smelling pink pomade stuff. Minnie had finished getting herself "gussied up"—she was wearing a shocking pink dress, a new pair of rhinestone glasses, and her hair, which she'd had done that very day, was very large and totally immovable. They told Benjamin that he could stay up until midnight, but to go to bed right afterwards. Ernie said they'd be home about one, and they left the telephone number of where they'd be, just in case there were any emergencies. They left the house at seven-thirty.

Benjamin took his pizza and salad into his room and turned on the television. He watched a few shows, but Thursday wasn't a great night for television, at least for shows Benjamin liked. He ate the entire pizza, finished the salad, and had some cookies for dessert. He then went through his 45s, picked out many of his favorites and put them on the record player, so they'd play one after another. He took out his Word Notebook and read through it. He took out his Encyclopedia of Strange Things and read through that, too. He read his Kritzerland musings. He read Susan Pomeroy's goodbye letter, and looked at the Penny Arcade photos of the two of them, where they were happily smiling together, the moment forever frozen in time.

As each of the records plunked down, he listened to *Young Love, Guess Things Happen That Way, Qué Será Será, When the Red Red Robin Comes Bob Bob Bobbin' Along,* and all the others that he'd loved, and he thought about all the things he'd been through. He thought about Grandpa Kritzer (whom he missed), he thought about his Commando Cody Rocket Jacket (which he'd outgrown), but mostly he thought about Susan. Benjamin had grown a bit taller in the two years since he'd seen her and he wondered if she had changed as well. He hoped she was happy and doing all right in far-off Montreal, Canada.

High Hopes dropped down on the record player.

Next time you're found with your chin on the ground
There's a lot to be learned, so look around

Benjamin's chin *had* been on the ground a few times, he'd gone through some rough spots, but he'd always managed to bounce back and be his unique and special self.

Just what makes that little old ant
Think he'll move that rubber tree plant
Anyone knows an ant can't
Move a rubber tree plant

No matter how hard or bleak things had been, Benjamin was just like that ant—he'd always managed to move the rubber tree plant. He was twelve now, his last year before he would become a teenager.

But he's got high hopes
He's got high hopes
He's got high apple pie in the sky hopes

Yes, Benjamin Kritzer had high hopes. He couldn't imagine where the 1960s would take him or what new dangers and adventures lay ahead; but whatever it was he would get through it with high apple pie in the sky hopes.

So, any time you're gettin' low
'Stead of lettin' go
Just remember that ant
Whoops, there goes another rubber tree plant

At 11:45, Benjamin went to the kitchen and made himself a grape Fizzie to toast in the New Year. He could hear a party going on in one of the neighboring houses; music was playing and people were laughing and yelling and

121

being rambunctious. Benjamin brought the Fizzie back to his room, turned off the light and waited for midnight. He didn't mean to fall asleep but he did, with *High Hopes* repeating itself on the record player, and the Penny Arcade photos of Susan and him gently resting in his hand.

PART TWO
1960

"Wherever we go,
Whatever we do,
We're gonna go through it together"

—*Together, Wherever We Go from Gypsy*

Bruce Kimmel

CHAPTER ONE

Paul Daley

The heater was on the fritz. Benjamin knew the heater was on the fritz because when he woke up the house was freezing. January had started off with unusually cold weather for Los Angeles, with temperatures in the mid-fifties. Normally, Benjamin liked the feel of cold sheets; he liked to snuggle beneath them, rubbing his feet against each other to keep them nice and toasty. But no amount of snuggling and rubbing was going to warm his feet because his feet were like ice cubes.

He got out of bed, shuddered from the chill in the air, and walked to the kitchen. Minnie was there, dressed in her usual pink quilt robe and pink slippers, hair, as usual, in curlers. What wasn't usual was that she was also wearing her full-length mink coat, and the image of her dressed like that made Benjamin rub his sleepy eyes in disbelief. He

125

then burst out laughing. Minnie looked up at him and said, "What are you laughing at? It's freezing—this is the only way to stay warm." Her false teeth were actually clattering in her mouth.

"Well, you look amusing," Benjamin replied, sitting down at the breakfast table. "Why is it so cold?"

"Because the heater is on the fritz," Minnie said, cracking an egg against the frying pan.

"The heater is on the fritz? What's a fritz?"

"*The* fritz, not *a* fritz. The heater is on *the* fritz."

"Okay, what's *the* fritz?"

Minnie was pushing the eggs around the frying pan in a kind of frenzy, as if that would somehow make her warmer. "The fritz is 'broken'," she said.

"The heater is on the fritz and the fritz is broken?" Benjamin asked, totally confused. He went to the refrigerator and poured himself some orange juice.

"You know what I mean, Benjamin. The fritz means broken," Minnie said, looking at Benjamin with daggers in her eyes.

"So, the heater is broken?"

"Yes, it's on the fritz, how many times do I have to tell you?"

"Why don't you just say it's broken?"

"Because I like saying it's on the fritz. Let me just say *this* to you, Benjamin. *You're* going to be on the fritz if you don't shut up. The heating man is coming at five to fix it."

Jeffrey came into the kitchen, yawning. "It's freezing."

Benjamin turned to his brother and said, "The heater is on the fritz."

Jeffrey belched loudly. Ernie came into the kitchen, wearing his usual pajama top and nothing else. "Why isn't the heater on, for God's sake?"

"It's on the fritz," Benjamin said.

"On the what?" Ernie replied, rubbing his hands together.

Minnie turned to the assembled Kritzers and started screaming. "The fritz, the fritz, are you all nuts?"

Benjamin thought that was a curious question coming from someone standing in the middle of the kitchen scrambling eggs while wearing a full-length mink coat. Minnie looked at Ernie with a sneer and continued screaming, "If you're so cold why don't you put some pants on for God's sake? You make me nauseous. What did I do to deserve a family like this?" Minnie then threw some scrambled eggs on everyone's plates and they all had breakfast in silence.

The upside of the heater being on the fritz was that Minnie decided to take Benjamin to the movies, where it would at least be warmer. When she asked Benjamin what he wanted to see, he, of course, said, *"Ben-Hur."*

"Ben-Hur, Ben-Hur, what is that, the only movie in the world? Fine, we'll go see *Ben-Hur*—anything to get out of this God-forsaken house."

They left the God-forsaken house at noon. Benjamin sat in the Cadillac, twirling the tuning knob on the radio, until he found something he liked—the theme from some movie called *A Summer Place.* Minnie didn't like other drivers and the entire trip up to Hollywood was peppered with comments like, "Look at that idiot, he never learned how to signal?" "C'mon already, are you going to a funeral?" and Benjamin's favorite, "Watch out, you son-of-a-bitch, pardon my French."

She drove up La Brea and turned right onto Hollywood Boulevard. They drove past the Grauman's Chinese and the Paramount, past Highland, and then there, on the right, was the beautiful Egyptian Theater. Minnie parked in a lot on Las Palmas, and they walked to the theater from there. There was a small line at the box-office. When it was their turn, they went up to the window and Minnie asked for two tickets. Unfortunately, *Ben-Hur* was playing reserved seats only, and all they had left was the first row, two seats over on the right side. She bought the tickets, which were quite expensive. The movie didn't start until two o'clock, so they went down the street and had lunch at Coffee Dan's. Benjamin had his favorite—the Dodger burger with french fries and a huge half-head of lettuce with Roquefort dressing on it. Minnie had a tuna fish sandwich and spent the whole meal complaining that it wasn't as good as *her* tuna fish sandwiches.

After lunch, they went back to the Egyptian and went in. The lobby was ornate and beautiful. Benjamin looked at the long staircase and really wanted to roll down those beautiful stairs, but he decided not to embarrass his mother, who he knew would react poorly. Benjamin really wanted a souvenir program but Minnie said it was too expensive on top of the too expensive tickets.

Inside, the theater was packed. They were shown to their first-row side seats. The curtained screen loomed large in front of them. Benjamin had never sat this close to the screen before, but he figured he would endure it to see *Ben-Hur*. He turned around and looked and the entire theater was filled. This was all very exciting—*Ben-Hur* was filmed in something called Camera 65, and that meant that it was bigger than Cinemascope. The curtained screen didn't look like it would be as big as Cinerama, but it was still huge and the burgundy curtains were quite beautiful.

At exactly two o'clock the lights dimmed and music began playing really loudly. The music was very dramatic and Benjamin liked it very much, especially the fact that it seemed to come from all over the theater. After about five minutes, the curtains opened to reveal a huge screen. The M-G-M lion roared and Benjamin could not believe how close they were to it. Because they were on the side everything seemed a little distorted, and it was very difficult to take in everything that was happening. Because of that, Benjamin had a little trouble following the story.

It seemed to be about two friends who became enemies because the girlfriend of one of the friends dropped a brick on someone. The mean friend who was now an enemy, made life miserable for Ben-Hur, and the girlfriend and her mother were put in jail for dropping the brick. After a while someone visited them in the jail cell and took one look at them, reacted with horror, and called them lepers. The girlfriend and her mother who were now lepers were then carted off to what they called a leper colony which was a valley where lepers had to live. As far as Benjamin could tell, lepers were people with icky stuff on their faces—in fact, it looked to Benjamin like lepers had wads of chewing gum all over their face.

There was an intermission and Minnie finally succumbed and bought Benjamin the too expensive program. Minnie was getting a migraine from the loud sound and being so close to the screen, and having to crane her neck upwards to watch the movie.

The second half was very exciting and had a wonderful chariot race. Watching the chariot race from the first row was like being there—it seemed like the chariots were going to run over the entire first row, including Benjamin and Minnie. At the end of it, the mean man got dragged by the chariots (served him right, Benjamin thought) and it was quite bloody and disgusting-looking (especially from the first row). Then there was some stuff about Jesus Christ, and then the lepers magically got cured and all the wads of chewing gum on their faces cleared up and they were fine-looking people once again.

The movie had been almost four hours long and it was dark when they came out of the theater. By the time they got home it was almost seven. As they walked in the door they were greeted with glorious heat. The heating man had come (Ernie had come home from work early to be there), and apparently he'd fixed the heater and now it was no longer on the fritz. The Kritzers all went out to Casa Cienega, where Benjamin had cheese enchiladas and rice and beans.

The next day, Benjamin used some Christmas money and bought the soundtrack to *Ben-Hur*, which came in a big box that included the same souvenir book Minnie had already bought him. He now had two souvenir books, so he cut one of them up and put the pictures on his bulletin board with little cut-out curtains around them, so that it looked like they were being shown in a movie theater.

* * *

Christmas vacation ended and Benjamin found himself back in the perplexing world of Louis Pasteur Junior High

School. He found it astonishing that in less than a month he'd be in the second half of the seventh grade, A7. He'd already been at Pasteur for five months.

Benjamin had his routine down and he rarely varied from it. He went from class to class, endured Gym (and Butch Polsky, who had become worse since Christmas vacation—constantly baiting Benjamin and purposely shoving him at every opportunity), and sitting in his various classrooms, eyes on the clock, counting the minutes until school was over.

In Wood Shop, Mr. Godowsky continued to pelt misbehaving boys with erasers, but luckily Benjamin had avoided the flying projectiles. They'd had projects to make, but Benjamin just couldn't get the hang of drills and dowels and sanding, and his projects looked totally unlike anyone else's and did not resemble in any way, shape or form what the project was supposed to look like. Therefore, Benjamin called his Wood Shop projects Benjamin's Mutant Bits of Wood.

One day, Benjamin was in the cafeteria eating macaroni and cheese when Butch Polsky came up to him. Benjamin looked up, mid-bite, and saw the crew-cut troublemaker glaring at him.

"It's bad enough I have to see your ugly face in Gym—I don't want to see it in this cafeteria anymore," sneered Butch, in his nasal voice.

Since this was the first time Benjamin had seen Butch Polsky in the cafeteria, he thought it strange that Butch had suddenly appointed himself boss of the cafeteria and that he was now telling people (like Benjamin) what to do. Benjamin swallowed the macaroni and cheese that was in his mouth, and replied in his best Grandpa Gelfinbaum voice, "What is it, fish?" Butch stood there, obviously unaware what a non-sequitur was.

"What did you say to me, creep?"

"What is it, fish?" Benjamin repeated.

"What is that supposed to mean?"

"Well, I think it's supposed to mean 'what is it, fish'. I guess it could mean something else—I guess it could mean 'why are you bothering me all the time'."

Butch's face suddenly had the appearance of a cast-iron skillet. "Listen to me—I don't want to see you in here again. I see you in here again and I'll beat the crap out of you."

Butch was moving closer to the table. Benjamin was trying to figure out what to do—he wondered if he should call out for help, or maybe pelt him with a Jell-O square, when suddenly he heard a voice from behind Butch.

"I'm afraid you won't be beating the crap out of anyone."

"Oh, yeah?" Butch replied belligerently, and turned around, only to find himself staring into the face of Mr. Hawkins, the Boys' Vice Principal. "Come with me, Mr. Polsky. Now." Butch was apoplectic. He turned around and glared at Benjamin, as if Benjamin had somehow caused the problem. Benjamin waved at him as Mr. Hawkins escorted Butch out of the cafeteria. Benjamin breathed a sigh of relief that the confrontation was over.

Standing near where Mr. Hawkins had been was a boy who was smiling, holding a lunch tray. Benjamin recognized the smiling boy from his Gym class. "I hate that guy", said the smiling boy. Then the smiling boy walked over to the table Benjamin was sitting at.

"Can I sit here?"

"Sure," said Benjamin. Anyone who hated Butch Polsky was okay with Benjamin.

The smiling boy put his lunch tray on the table and sat down. "The minute I saw what that oaf was doing I got Mr. Hawkins."

Benjamin liked that word "oaf". "Well, thanks. I didn't know what to do. He's crazy, that oaf. That oaf has been giving me a hard time since the first day I started school. What's an oaf?"

"An oaf? I don't know, like a fool, a jerk, a dope. My mother calls everyone an oaf, including me. I'm Paul. Paul Daley."

"I'm Benjamin. Benjamin Kritzer. We're in Gym class together—I'm the one who can't play baseball, football, volleyball, basketball or any other sport known to man."

Paul Daley laughed. It was a loud boisterous laugh and quite infectious, and it made Benjamin laugh, too. Soon they were relating their separate tales of junior high school horror to each other, as they finished their lunch. The bell rang and they got up to deposit their trash and put their trays down.

"Want to have lunch tomorrow?" Paul asked.

"Sure."

"Great," said Paul Daley. "Tomorrow we can figure out who else in this cafeteria is an oaf."

"We'll be oaf hunters. I've always called oafs foorps."

They began walking towards the exit. "What's a foorp?" asked Paul Daley.

"I made it up. It's 'proof' spelled backwards. It means idiots. Foorps are oafs."

"Then we'll be the foorp and oaf hunters of Louis Pasteur Junior High School." Paul Daley laughed his boisterous laugh as he and Benjamin went off to their respective classes.

* * *

The next day, the foorp and oaf hunters of Louis Pasteur Junior High met at the cafeteria. They said hello and got their trays and stood in line. Benjamin got Shepherd's Pie and Jell-O squares, Paul got meatloaf and mashed potatoes and yellow pudding. They sat at the same table as they had the day before. As they ate and talked, they began to try and identify the various foorps and oafs sitting in the cafeteria. Eventually, they'd identified every single person as a foorp or oaf (except themselves, of course)—although they exempted two pretty girls who were sitting together, because it looked like they too were trying to identify foorps and oafs.

Over the next week, Benjamin and Paul ate lunch together in the cafeteria every day. Benjamin told Paul all about his family, how his parents were Martians, how his brother was psychotic, how his grandfather always said, "What is it, fish?" and lots of other details about the Kritzer household.

In return, Benjamin learned that Paul had a mother, Esther, and a beatnik sister, Fran. Paul's mother had booted out his father when Paul was five, because his father was a no-goodnik, at least according to his mother. The Daleys lived at the corner of Garth and Airdrome (a block from where Susan had lived) in a modest Spanish-style house which Benjamin had walked by many times on his way to Crescent Heights and Pasteur. The Daleys also had very little money and surviving was always a struggle. Paul would barely have enough money to buy his lunch, and when Benjamin asked him if he wanted to go to the movies with him, Paul had declined because he'd spent all of his allowance that week. Considering that Paul could barely pay for his lunch every day, he was quite beefy, not fat exactly, but definitely on the chubby side.

Having a new friend was interesting for Benjamin. He'd never really had a *friend* friend (except for Susan, and she was so much more than that, that the word "friend" didn't really apply to her), even though he'd thought it would be nice to have one. It was just that he'd always found most other people his age to be insufferable, so he'd kept to himself. But Paul was different—Paul had a sense of humor and seemed to understand the way Benjamin's mind worked. Paul was smart, and he had that funny boisterous laugh which always made Benjamin laugh.

At one of their lunches, Benjamin posed a key question.

"Do you like *The Twilight Zone?*" Benjamin asked, playing with his Tuna Surprise.

"I've only seen it once. I really liked it, it was creepy. But we only have one television in the house and my mother likes to watch *People are Funny.*"

"I can't believe you've only seen it once. I never miss it—every Friday night I get spaghetti and meatballs from Scarantino's and watch it in my bedroom with all the lights off."

"You have a television in your bedroom?"

"Yeah, we got it for Christmas. I share a room with my psycho brother, but he's not around much these days. He's in some club now and all they do is drink Ripple. He comes home now and then and throws up. That's the only time we see him. He comes home, throws up in the toilet and goes out again."

A few days later, Benjamin asked Minnie if his new friend Paul could come over to have dinner and watch *The Twilight Zone* on Friday night.

"You have a friend?" Minnie asked.

"Yes, I have a friend. What am I, a leper? I couldn't have a friend?"

"I didn't say you were a leper, Benjamin. I was surprised, that's all. It's not exactly like you've had a ton of friends now, is it?"

"Well, can my friend come over and watch *The Twilight Zone*? We can get Scarantino's."

Minnie eyed Benjamin suspiciously. "There's nothing strange about your friend, is there?"

"Strange? You mean does he have two noses or something?"

"You know what I mean, Benjamin. Is he a hoodlum?"

"Is he a hoodlum?"

"Is there an echo in here? Is he a hoodlum or is he a nice boy?"

"He's a nice boy. He's Jewish and everything. Do they have Jewish hoodlums?"

"As long as he's not a hoodlum he can come over."

As Benjamin turned to leave, Minnie snapped at him, "A thank you would be nice."

"Thank you," Benjamin replied, in his nicest Benjamin voice.

Outside, the Helms truck sounded its whistle and Benjamin scurried outside to get himself a chocolate donut.

* * *

The following Friday, Benjamin walked over to Paul's house so they could walk up to Scarantino's, get their food, and then walk back to Benjamin's house. He knocked on the door and it was answered by a twenty-year-old girl with the blackest hair Benjamin had ever seen. She had dark circles under her eyes and was wearing a beret.

"Yeah," she said by way of a greeting.

"Is Paul here?" Benjamin asked. He couldn't take his eyes off this strange creature.

"Yeah, man, come in. He's in his room, I'll get him."

Benjamin went in the house and stood in the living room while the beret-wearing black-haired girl went off to get Paul. The room was furnished sparsely, with nothing that really matched. The sofa was burgundy with a floral pattern on it. There was a beige armchair nearby, a coffee table that had seen better days, and a television set plopped up against one wall, with a rabbit-ears antenna sitting on top.

The girl came back in the room. "He'll be here in a second, man. Who are you?"

"I'm Benjamin."

"Oh, yeah, man, Benjamin, he mentioned you. I'm Fran, his sister."

Benjamin smiled at her, while trying to figure out why she said "man" so much. Perhaps that was part of being what Paul had called a "beatnik". She wasn't exactly a female version of Maynard G. Krebs, the only other beatnik Benjamin had ever seen (on the TV show, *Dobie Gillis*, which he never missed); she seemed very serious with a permanent furrow in her brow, as if she were always fretting about something-or-other. A voice called out from the kitchen—"Frannie, who is it?"

Fran gave a dirty look to the kitchen and said, "It's Paul's new friend, Benjamin." She turned to Benjamin. "I hate when she calls me Frannie, man. That is tremendously retarded in my opinion. She's from squaresville, in my opinion. Have you ever read any Ginsberg?"

Benjamin, trying to keep up with this exotic new language replied, "Ginsberg?" Benjamin didn't have a clue who Ginsberg was—to Benjamin, Ginsberg sounded like a rabbi or someone who worked at a delicatessen.

"You should, he's the coolest—he's a poet. Read his stuff, you'll dig him. Very profound, very meaningful."

Benjamin didn't know from poetry, profound or otherwise. Fran kept staring at him, her eyes like black pools boring into him, and it made Benjamin feel like he was under a microscope.

A gray-haired woman emerged from the kitchen. "You're Benjamin?" she asked. "It's nice to meet you. I'm Paul's mother."

"Hi," Benjamin said, and smiled politely.

"I see you've met Frannie."

"Mother, can you please cool it with Frannie? You are really irking me." Fran left the room. Paul's mother turned to Benjamin. "I'm irking her. Go know. So, Benjamin, do you know how to do the Limbo?"

Benjamin was beginning to wonder if there was actually a family that was stranger than his own. Before he could answer the Limbo question, Paul came into the room. "Hi, sorry, I was in the bathroom."

His mother made a tsking sound, and said, "So nice of you to let us all know. Such an oaf. I was asking Benjamin if he knew how to do the Limbo."

"If he doesn't, I'm sure you'll show him," Paul said, and then he pushed Benjamin toward the front door. "Let's get out of here, before she puts on the Limbo record."

As Paul opened the door, Benjamin turned to Paul's mother and said, "Nice to meet you, Mrs. Daley."

"Nice to meet you, too, Benjamin. Next time you're here, we'll do the Limbo." She smiled, as Paul nudged Benjamin out the door.

"That's my family," said Paul, laughing his boisterous laugh, as he and Benjamin walked toward La Cienega.

At Scarantino's, Benjamin bought both of them spaghetti and meatballs and an order of garlic bread. As they walked back towards Benjamin's house, they discussed everything they saw—the miniature golf course, Fosters Freeze, Marty's Bike and Candy Shop, the Adohr bottling plant, absolutely everything. Paul didn't frequent as many of those places as Benjamin did, but he was very intrigued by Benjamin's stories of playing on the Adohr trucks that had been put out to pasture. Unfortunately, no one would be playing on those trucks anymore, because the Adohr bottling plant was closed and going to be torn down to make way for a new A&P market.

They got back to Benjamin's house at around eight. As they walked down the hallway, Minnie's voice rang out from the den. "Aren't you going to introduce your new friend?"

Benjamin suddenly had a vision of his father sitting in his easy chair wearing only his pajama top and he didn't know whether to warn Paul or just hope that his father still had his pants on. He gestured for Paul to follow him into the den.

Mercifully, Ernie had his pants on. Minnie looked over at Paul and said, "Hello, Paul."

Paul nodded and replied, "Hello, Mrs. Kritzer."

Minnie gestured towards Ernie. "This is Benjamin's father."

Ernie swiveled around and said, "Hello, Paul."

Again, Paul nodded and replied, "Hello, Mr. Kritzer."

Benjamin waited to see if there was going to be any further lively conversation, but it appeared that the meeting was over. "Okay, we're going to my room to eat."

"Don't make a mess. Don't get food all over everything. Don't forget the napkins. Eat over your plates and don't spill."

Benjamin ushered Paul out of the den, as Minnie continued her litany of don'ts. They went into the bedroom. There were no chairs there, so they had to sit on the beds, Benjamin on his own, Paul on Jeffrey's. While they ate their spaghetti and meatballs, and their garlic bread, Benjamin showed Paul his Word Notebook, his *Ben-Hur* bulletin board, his Encyclopedia of Strange Things, and a few of his magic tricks. Paul was a willing audience and seemed duly impressed. After they finished their dinner, Benjamin got out his Jerry Mahoney dummy and did his entire Fine and Dandy routine, which Paul laughed at continuously.

Finally, it was ten o'clock and time for *The Twilight Zone*. Benjamin turned on the television and then turned off the lights and waited for *Desilu Playhouse* to finish. He brought Paul up to date on some of the creepier *Twilight Zones* that Paul had missed, and that put them in the mood for whatever creepy episode was going to unfold that very evening. Of course, the wonderful thing about *The Twilight Zone* was that it had a new story every week, so you never knew what you were going to get.

The eerie theme came on, and he and Paul nibbled on the rest of their spaghetti and meatballs while they watched the story, which was called *The Hitchhiker*. It was about a woman driving and everywhere she looked she saw this creepy man who was trying to hitch a ride. No matter how far she drove, there he was, hitching a ride. Finally, at the end, the woman calls home in desperation, only to find out that she (the woman) had died in a car crash the night before. On the news of that little revelation, Benjamin and Paul simultaneously looked at each other with ever-widening eyes. That little revelation was just bone-chilling, in Benjamin's opinion. The hitchhiker then came up to her and said, "Going my way?" Benjamin had goose bumps on his arms and again he and Paul looked at each other with expressions of dread on their faces. As the credits came on, they couldn't stop talking about the show and how scary it was and how they both liked the pretty blonde lady, Inger Stevens.

After the show, they took their plates to the kitchen and put them in the sink. They could hear Ernie snoring loudly from the den. Minnie came in and said she'd drive Paul home.

They got into the Cadillac and drove the few blocks to Paul's house. Benjamin went with Paul to the door and instead of saying good night, he opened his eyes wide, looked at Paul with a weird expression, put out his thumb like the hitchhiker had and said, "Going my way?" The two of them burst out laughing, as Paul went inside and Benjamin went back to the car.

* * *

During the next few days at school, whenever Benjamin and Paul would see each other on the schoolyard or at lunch, they would always stick out their thumbs like the hitchhiker, and say, "Going my way?" and then laugh loudly. The other kids who saw them do this over and over again began to look at them as if they'd escaped from a mental institution.

The next Friday night they repeated what was to be their *Twilight Zone* ritual—dinner from Scarantino's and sitting in the dark watching the latest episode from ten to ten-thirty. That night, the episode was called *The Fever*, and was about an uptight man and his wife in Las Vegas. The man thinks gambling is evil, but he ends up gambling anyway, and then the slot machines start calling his name—"Franklin"—accompanied by the sound of coins dropping. The slot machine ends up coming to Franklin's hotel room (all in his crazy mind, of course) and Franklin ends up falling out the window.

The next week at school, instead of the hitchhiker's "Going my way?" it was "Franklin" said over and over, in a voice approximating the way the slot machine had sounded in the show.

One day, Benjamin was in Wood Shop. Class hadn't begun yet and Benjamin was standing by one of the open windows. Suddenly, Paul walked by and said loudly, "Franklin, Franklin, Franklin" in that slot machine voice— Benjamin turned and said, "Going my way?" in return, and as he did so, an eraser whizzed by his face and out the window, clipping Paul a good one on the side of the head. They talked about *that* for days.

* * *

February arrived and Benjamin found himself going into the second half of the seventh grade, A7. He couldn't believe it—he'd already been at the school almost six months. His report card was decent, mostly C's with the occasional B, and an A in English. His cooperation and work habits marks were all S's—satisfactory, no U's—unsatisfactory, and three E's—excellent. All in all, not a bad report card. Best of all, he had a friend, and he was now spending most of his time doing things with Paul—watching *The Twilight Zone* every week, seeing movies (he'd shown Paul his amazing falling-down-the-stairs business, and Paul had tried to emulate him and had almost broken his neck), and walking around the neighborhood. They were beginning to be like a team—like Abbott and Costello, with Paul the straight man and Benjamin the funny man. Butch Polsky still gave Benjamin murderous looks in Gym class, but whatever Mr. Hawkins had said or done to him had stopped Butch from tormenting him.

In A7, Benjamin no longer had to endure Wood Shop. That class had been replaced by Music Appreciation, which Benjamin was looking forward to. He especially liked his teacher, Mr. Williamson, who was very thin (his pants always seemed like they were going to fall off) and pale, with a full head of red hair which seemed to go in all directions at once. Mr. Williamson was passionate about music and promised the class they were going to go on many musical journeys. Since Benjamin loved music, he was quite certain he would love Music Appreciation.

The third week of February, Benjamin was in his room watching *American Bandstand*, when he noticed some red spots on his arm. He looked at his other arm and there were red spots there, too. He looked at the palm of his hands and, although they were faint, he could see a few there. He wondered if he'd gotten bitten by a mosquito or gnat or something. He went into the bathroom, and noticed three red spots on his face, which hadn't been there that morning. He then walked into the kitchen and held his arm up to Minnie and said, "What are these?"

Minnie took one look at his arm, then looked at his face, and then hit herself in the forehead with the palm of her hand. "You've got measles," Minnie said in a pinched tone. "Where on earth did you get measles?"

"The measles store?" Benjamin replied. "How do I know where I got measles?"

"Well, you got them somewhere because you have them. Someone at school must have given them to you."

"Can I give them back?" Benjamin asked, scratching his arm.

Minnie slapped his hand and said, "Don't scratch. You're not supposed to scratch. Now, you get right into bed and that's where you'll stay for a week, maybe two. I'll call the school tomorrow."

"I have to stay in bed for a week, maybe two? Just because of some spots?"

Minnie looked at Benjamin with wide eyes. "People have *died* from the measles! Get in bed now. And don't scratch."

Benjamin went into his room and undressed, got in his pajamas and hopped into bed. He noticed there were a few red spots on his feet and legs now. Minnie made him soup and brought it to him on a tray. Luckily, Jeffrey had already had the measles (apparently Jeffrey hadn't died from them) and so he couldn't get them again. Benjamin called Paul to tell him the measles news—as it turned out, Paul had already had them, too (apparently Paul hadn't died from them either), and so he could come over and visit. Benjamin sat in bed, head propped up against a pillow, watching television, and wondered why everyone seemed to have had the measles but him.

By bedtime, Benjamin was covered with red spots from head to toe.

CHAPTER TWO

Measles, Music Appreciation, and Kritzer and Daley

The next morning, Dr. Hallberg came to the house and ascertained that Benjamin did indeed have the measles. He took Benjamin's temperature and it was one hundred. He told Benjamin and Minnie that the measles would last approximately two weeks, and the only thing to do was get plenty of rest.

Benjamin could not believe what he looked like. He was a mass of red spots—it was as if someone had poured a box of Red Hots all over him. Benjamin did not like being sick and he most definitely did not like the measles. He itched like crazy but Minnie had warned him not to scratch. Well, was there anything worse than someone telling you not to scratch when you itched? That just made you itch twice as much, didn't it? On the other hand, Benjamin didn't have to go to school for two weeks, and Paul, who'd already had the measles, could come over after school and keep him company; although Minnie said it would have to be in a few days as she thought Benjamin should just rest and get his temperature down first.

The doctor had said to keep the room dark (apparently, light was not good for the measles), so the blinds were drawn twenty-four hours a day.

Benjamin mostly watched television and slept. He ate poached eggs on toast for breakfast, chicken noodle soup for lunch, and whatever was for dinner for dinner. He watched *Chef Milani*, *Chucko's Cartoons*, *Ramar*, and he also began watching the morning quiz shows. In fact, he became obsessed with the morning quiz shows—*Dough Re Mi*, *Treasure Hunt*, *Price is Right*, *Concentration*, *Truth or Consequences*—he rooted for the people he liked, tried to figure out the answers to each question, and decided he wanted to be a quiz show host, all the while trying not to scratch.

There was nothing really good on from two to four, so he got a bunch of magazines from the den to look at. He thumbed through them, checking out the photos, not really reading anything. In one of the *Look* magazines he found an ad for something called The Columbia Record Club. According to the ad, if you joined The Columbia Record Club for one year, and purchased just one album a month, you could get your very own personal stereophonic record player for $9.99. It was a compact model with swing-out speakers, which could be detached if you happened to be in a detaching mood. The Kritzers didn't own a stereophonic record player—the player/television console in the den was monaural. Now that Benjamin had seen a picture of a stereophonic record player (the ad said the sound was so lifelike that it was almost like being there—wherever "there" was), he could no longer make do with a dreary old monaural record player. He simply had to have his very own stereophonic record player with detachable speakers.

When he showed Minnie the ad, her first response was "Go play in traffic." Benjamin told her he couldn't play in traffic as he had the measles. He also told her that if he had his very own Columbia House Stereophonic Record Player with detachable speakers that he would do extra chores around the house and that it would also make his measles get better faster, and he would be less prone to scratching.

"It's only ten dollars," Benjamin implored in his best I'm-so-sick-with-the-measles voice.

"Only ten dollars. Money doesn't grow on trees, you know," Minnie replied. "And besides, you have to buy a record a month for a year."

"I'll pay for it out of my allowance, I promise."

"You are a spoiled rotten child, Benjamin, and you don't need a record player. Shut up and eat your soup."

"But they deliver it in a week, if you ask for a rush," he said, holding up the *Look* magazine ad. "It doesn't cost extra, and it's COD. I could have it while I've still got the measles. A whole record player for ten dollars, how can we pass up an offer like that?"

"By saying no," Minnie said, growing weary of the discussion.

Knowing she was growing weary of the discussion and therefore would be susceptible to deciding he could have it, he pressed on. "It could be an early birthday present."

"Your birthday's not for ten months."

"So, it could be a really *early* birthday present."

"Benjamin, why must you have everything you see? Every time you open a magazine or see something in the store, you have to have it."

"Not really. I don't need Geritol for iron-poor blood. I don't need a Remington Electric Shaver for a smoother shave. Besides, I'm sick with the measles. I'd feel better with a stereophonic record player."

Minnie breathed a long sigh and said, "Oy, why couldn't I have a normal child? Why was I blessed with an idiot? Fine, we'll order it, it's your measles present. But I better not see you scratch once, and you will be taking out the garbage for a year."

When Paul came over the next afternoon, Benjamin told him all about the impending delivery of his very own Columbia House Stereophonic Record Player with detachable speakers. It would arrive soon and it would include his first album selection. He'd had difficulty figuring out which album to choose, as he couldn't really tell what they were from just looking at the pictures of the covers. He'd finally settled on an album called *Gypsy*, the new hit Broadway musical. He didn't know anything about *Gypsy*, the new hit Broadway musical, but he liked the cover, and he'd always enjoyed the other Broadway albums in the house. In fact, he'd bought several Ed Sullivan albums, which featured songs from a variety of different Broadway musicals (only 99 cents at Daylight Market, a bargain in Benjamin's opinion—a whole album for the same price as a 45).

Paul filled him in on the various goings on at school, and said that several people had asked where Benjamin was, including Glenda Allen, the girl who'd told him to stop smiling at her. Paul couldn't stay too long as he had homework to do, but they watched *American Bandstand*, where they heard all the latest songs, none of which Benjamin liked very much.

* * *

Paul came over every afternoon at around three-fifteen. Benjamin, by this time, was bored out of his mind. It wasn't like he was on vacation—he couldn't go out, couldn't go to the movies, couldn't do anything but lie in bed and watch television and sleep. So, it was fun to have company every day, even though it was just for an hour or two.

On Wednesday, Lulu came to clean, took one look at Benjamin and cackled with delight, "Oh, my, my, my, you look like you been decorated with polka dots." Later she brought him a ham sandwich and cackled again, "Oh, my, my, my, I've never seen so many spots as that whole lot of spots on you, Benjamin Kritzer." That made Benjamin think that he sounded like some species of wildlife—the Spotted Benjamin.

Six days later, Benjamin's new Columbia House Stereophonic Record Player arrived in a big box. He couldn't get it open fast enough. Included in the box was his first selection, *Gypsy*. He took out the record player and looked at it. It was gray, with a kind of mottled finish to it. He undid the clasp of the lid and lifted it. It was a very nice stereophonic record player to Benjamin's eye, and it looked like it was very simple to operate. It played three speeds, 78, 45 and 33 1/3. It came with a little adaptor so one could play 45s on it, too. He plugged it into the wall socket near his bed, got under the covers and set the player on his lap. He undid the clasps of the two speakers on the left and right and swung them open.

It was compact, but to Benjamin it was very impressive-looking. He couldn't wait to hear the stereophonic sound (so lifelike that it was almost like being there)—he ripped off the plastic covering from the *Gypsy* album and carefully put the platter onto the turntable. He turned the volume up nice and loud (the door was closed), and moved the needle over to the record.

A moment later, something called the *Overture* began, the sound coming out of both speakers, in full glorious stereophonic sound. The instruments seemed to come from all over, some on the left, some in the middle and some on the right. It was very exciting, this panorama of sound, and Benjamin couldn't believe it. He was careful to keep very still so he didn't disturb the record player and cause the needle to slide. The first song, *Let Us Entertain You* was cute, he thought, and again, the voices came not just from the center like on the record player in the den, they came from the left and the middle and the right. And not only that, they *moved*. That was the most amazing thing of all—a voice would start out on the left, move to the middle and end up on the right. It really was so lifelike that it was almost like being there.

The next song was called *Some People* and Benjamin loved it immediately, especially the line, "Some people sit on their butts"—he just thought that was the funniest thing he ever heard in a song. Ricky Nelson didn't sing "Some people sit on their butts" nor did Elvis, or The Platters, or Teresa Brewer, or Tab Hunter or Bobby Darin, but Ethel Merman sang it and she sang it with gusto.

Benjamin had never ever heard a voice like Ethel Merman's. He'd seen her on the *Ed Sullivan Show* a few times, and liked her because she sang so loud. And now she was coming out of the two speakers on his lap and it was so lifelike it was not only like being there, it was like having Ethel Merman in the room with you. He played the rest of Side One, and every song was better than the last one. He played *Little Lamb* twice in a row, because it reminded him of Susan (he didn't know why, really, but it was so sweet and pretty, it just did). Side Two was just as good, but his absolute *favorite* favorite on the whole album was *Together, Wherever We Go*. He couldn't get the music out of his head, and he played it over and over again. He'd learned the words by heart within an hour, and he sang along with the record. It was also a perfect description of his friendship with Paul.

Wherever we go, whatever we do
We're gonna go through it together

Yes, that's what friendship was all about.

With you for me and me for you
We'll muddle through whatever we do
Together wherever we go

Didn't that just describe Benjamin and Paul to a "t"? After listening to *Gypsy* a few more times, Benjamin went to the den and rifled through the albums there, but they were all in monaural sound and, after hearing stereophonic sound, monaural sound would just not do at all.

Benjamin went back to his room and listened to *Gypsy* three more times, and when Paul came over that afternoon, he played it for him and Paul loved it, too, and was very impressed with the stereophonic sound.

A week later, Benjamin was done with the measles. The red spots disappeared as quickly as they'd come, and through it all, Benjamin had kept his promise and never scratched, not even once.

*   *   *

Back in school, Benjamin had some swift catching up to do, which he did as best he could. Paul was happy he was back, because it meant they could resume their recesses and lunches together.

By far, of all Benjamin's classes, he loved Music Appreciation most of all. He actually looked forward to it every day. Mr. Williamson was a wonderful teacher who spoke with such passion about the music he played that it was infectious, at least to Benjamin. The other students seemed fairly bored by it all—anything that wasn't rock-and-roll they couldn't be bothered with. Benjamin didn't understand why they couldn't like all kinds of music, but they just sat there with total indifference and that was their loss as far as Benjamin was concerned. Of course, that just meant Mr. Williamson played to Benjamin because he could see that Benjamin was so involved and immersed in the music.

Mr. Williamson liked to play a piece of classical music and have the students close their eyes and create what he called mind pictures, images that the music would conjure up. Benjamin loved doing that, creating mind pictures.

Certain music, he explained, was descriptive—the music would try to paint an aural picture. So, when Mr. Williamson played *The Moldau* by someone named Smetana, he told the students that the Moldau was a river and that the music was painting a picture of it. As the first strains of the music began, Benjamin closed his eyes and immediately was able to perfectly picture a river because that's exactly what that music conjured up, all swirling and majestic and flowing. Somehow that composer, Smetana, had captured in music the feeling of a river, and even though Benjamin had obviously never seen that river, his imagination, led by the music, enabled him to see his own version of it clearly.

When Mr. Williamson played Aaron Copland's *Appalachian Spring*, it was, to Benjamin's closed eyes, like being outdoors in a big open field, where everything smelled clean and sweet and where you could see for miles and miles with crystal clarity. It was almost as if the music cleared your sinuses, you could breathe so clearly and easily.

When Mr. Williamson played Vaughan Williams' *Fantasia on Greensleeves*, Benjamin was transported to an English countryside, so green it hurt your eyes—with sheep and meadows and ponds, all courtesy of Vaughan Williams (and Mr. Williamson, of course). What green sleeves had to do with anything, Benjamin had no idea, but he still loved the gentle and haunting music.

Then there was non-descriptive music, and Mr. Williamson encouraged everyone to let that music take them wherever their minds would allow. When Mr. Williamson played Rachmaninov's *Symphony Number Two*—the third movement—the strangest thing happened. The music began, simple and radiantly beautiful. Benjamin closed his eyes, and suddenly, there he was, in Kritzerland.

He hadn't thought about Kritzerland in ages, yet there he was, in his perfect world, with Susan, walking and holding hands, the sunlight bouncing off her golden blonde hair blindingly. How could a composer (Rachmaninov) capture what was in Benjamin's head and heart? That was just the most astonishing thing, but somehow the music was doing just that, that beautiful melody bringing everything he'd pictured and dreamed of in Kritzerland to life.

Of course, he had to have all those albums, and he got them by telling his mother they were for his class. As long as she felt he was being studious, it was worth the $5.98 to Minnie. So, Benjamin got *Appalachian Spring*—he always made sure to get the same version that Mr. Williamson had played in class, because when he went to the store to buy it they had about ten different albums with that same piece of music (Benjamin got the one conducted by Leonard Bernstein). He got *The Moldau* (conducted by Eugene Ormandy), he got *Fantasia on Greensleeves* (conducted by Adrian Boult), and best of all, he got Rachmaninov's *Symphony Number Two*. He listened to them over and over again (especially the Rachmaninov) on his Columbia House Stereophonic Record Player, always with his eyes closed so he could let the music carry him away in a sea of wondrous images.

Benjamin began staying after school for fifteen minutes or so every day to hang out in Mr. Williamson's classroom, and those visits were the best, with Mr. Williamson going on rhapsodically about his favorite composers and his favorite music. Paul would come, too, because he, like Benjamin, also loved music. Sometimes during those after school visits, Mr. Williamson would play short pieces of music for Benjamin and Paul, things that he loved but that weren't part of his teaching plan. That's where Benjamin first heard *Warsaw Concerto* (which was actually from a film, Mr. Williamson said) with its opening crashing piano chords that led into a wonderfully romantic theme. Benjamin loved those opening crashing piano chords, and when he got home he immediately went to the piano and tried to emulate them. After several hours of cacophonous banging, Minnie finally came in the room with a look of pained annoyance. "Benjamin, are you trying to kill the piano?"

"I'm trying to play the *Warsaw Concerto*," Benjamin replied, as he continued slamming the keys, trying to find the right notes.

"Well, whatever you're doing, it's from hunger and I want you to knock it off. You don't know how to play the piano, that could be the first problem."

Benjamin continued banging away determinedly.

"Benjamin, I am warning you to stop that racket. Don't you have homework?"

"Yes, I have to learn how to play the *Warsaw Concerto*."

"You're going to *be* in Warsaw if you keep this up. Shut up, stop with the banging and go do something useful."

"This is useful."

"This is dreck," Minnie said, and then she began to yell. "Benjamin, enough with the *Warsaw Concerto*! If I hear one more bang out of you, you will not watch television for a week!"

That stopped Benjamin, but quick. Before either of them could say anything else, the front door opened and Ernie came in. He looked at Minnie and Benjamin at the piano and said, "What's going on?"

"Your son has been banging on the piano for two hours, that's what's going on," Minnie replied.

"Why are you banging on the piano and driving your mother crazy?" Ernie asked.

"I was trying to play the *Warsaw Concerto*," Benjamin answered.

Ernie's eyes lit up. "The *Warsaw Concerto?*"

"Yeah, I heard it in school."

"I've always loved the *Warsaw Concerto*," Ernie said, smiling.

Minnie looked at her husband as if he were a pile of bird droppings. "Oh, brother."

"You know the *Warsaw Concerto?*" Benjamin asked, not believing that a Martian parent could know such a thing.

"Of course I know the *Warsaw Concerto*, it's a wonderful piece of music," Ernie said, walking over to the piano.

Minnie watched Ernie walk over to the piano with disgust, and said, "Why don't the two of you drop dead with the *Warsaw Concerto?* You are both nauseating me."

Ernie gestured for Benjamin to move over and he sat down to his left and suddenly began playing something that almost sounded like the *Warsaw Concerto*. It wasn't right, but it was a reasonably close facsimile. Benjamin couldn't believe his father was able to play something that almost sounded like the *Warsaw Concerto*. Oh, he'd heard Ernie noodling at the piano, but this just came out of left field. Minnie stood there with her arms crossed, looking as if she'd just sucked on three lemons, and then she stormed back to the kitchen to resume cooking that evening's dinner of Pepper Steak.

Ernie showed Benjamin how to sort of play the *Warsaw Concerto*, and within fifteen minutes Benjamin had it down cold. There he was, playing the *Warsaw Concerto* (sort of), or at least the opening of the *Warsaw Concerto*, and he continued to do so until he heard Minnie screaming from the kitchen, "Hey, Van Cliburn, dinner is on the table!"

*   *   *

Now that Benjamin had a best friend (well, truth be told, an *only* friend), he decided it was time to take Paul to Ocean Park so he could meet Grandma and Grandpa Gelfinbaum. Benjamin had told him about Grandma Gelfinbaum's pinching of the cheeks and Grandpa's stools, and the "What is it, fish?" business. In fact, that had become a key bit in the daily routines of the new comedy team of Kritzer and Daley. They said it constantly at school, much to the befuddlement of their classmates and teachers.

Minnie was busy and couldn't take them to Ocean Park on Saturday, so Benjamin and Paul decided to take the bus there. Benjamin showed up at Paul's house at ten in the morning and was greeted by Paul's mother, breathing heavily, standing in a bathrobe, while music played loudly in the background.

"Hello, Benjamin. I was practicing the Twist. Paul will be out in a minute, he's just brushing his teeth. I'm making oatmeal, do you want some?" Mrs. Daley asked, as she went over to the record player and shut the music off.

"No, thank you," Benjamin said.

"Have you done the Twist?" she asked.

"What's the Twist?"

"It's a great new song. I heard it on *American Bandstand*. It's gonna be a big hit."

"You watch *American Bandstand?*" Benjamin asked, rather surprised.

Mrs. Daley looked at Benjamin for a moment and then replied, "Yes, I watch *American Bandstand.* Just because I have prematurely gray hair doesn't mean I'm old and not with it. You've got to learn the Twist, it's so much fun."

She turned the record back on and began doing a very strange dance, hips moving every which way and her arms moving in some wild, weird counterpoint to her twisting hips.

"C'mon, it's fun. I'm telling you, it's gonna be a number one hit—I know these things. Chubby Checker, he's great!"

Luckily, Benjamin was saved from doing the Twist because a door opened and Paul's sister Fran, the beatnik, came down the hallway and into the living room. She had a black eye mask on, which was up on her forehead, as if she'd just lifted it up there so she could see where she was going, and she was wearing a black t-shirt which barely covered her black underpants which Benjamin, of course, couldn't help but stare at. Fran looked sleepily at Benjamin, saw him staring and said, "Hey, man, what are you looking at?"

"Look who's up early," Mrs. Daley said, noticing Fran. To Benjamin she said, "She usually can't be bothered to get up before noon." To Fran she said, "Want some oatmeal, Frannie?"

"Oatmeal? What am I, five? Who can sleep with that stupid music playing? Coffee, man, I need coffee."

"Don't start with the 'man', Frannie."

"Don't start with the 'Frannie', man."

"The way she talks, it's such a cliché. Man this, man that. It's ridiculous if you ask me."

"This from a woman doing the Twist. Man."

Paul came bounding down the hallway, saw Benjamin and said, "Let's go."

Mrs. Daley waved at Paul and said, "I was showing Benjamin how to Twist. Paul's quite a good Twister. Show him, Paul."

"We have to go," Paul said hurriedly.

"Fine, party-pooper. Have fun. Don't get home too late."

Paul ushered Benjamin out the front door quickly, as Chubby Checker kept on telling everyone to Twist again like we did last summer.

They walked up La Cienega to Pico and caught the bus to Santa Monica. It was the first time Benjamin had ever taken a bus to the beach. Even though the bus took the exact same route as the Kritzers did when they drove, it seemed like a totally different ride.

The bus let them off at Main and Pico. They walked south to Kinney and then made their way to the St. Regis. They took the rickety elevator up to the third floor. Paul was properly impressed by the *Twilight Zone*-ness of the creaky elevator (it could be taking them to the fourth dimension rather than the third floor), and certainly the musty and dimlit hallway was creepy, too, if you looked at it in the right frame of mind. When they neared the apartment, Paul looked at Benjamin, stuck out his thumb and said, "Going my way?" to which Benjamin replied, "What is it, fish?"

Benjamin knocked on the apartment door. From behind the door they heard Grandma Gelfinbaum's muffled voice

160

yelling, "Answer the door" followed by Grandpa Gelfinbaum's muffled voice yelling, "I'm watching Gene Autrey, you answer the door" followed by Grandma Gelfinbaum's voice yelling, "Oy gevalt, you're such a nudnik." The door opened and there was Grandma Gelfinbaum, dressed, as usual, all in black. She looked at Benjamin, then reached out and pinched his cheeks. "Look who's here? It's Benjamin."

From the other room, Grandpa Gelfinbaum could be heard hocking a glob of spit (heaven only knew *where* he was hocking it) after which he said, "I'm watching Gene Autrey. Stop bothering me."

"Hi, Grandma. This is my friend Paul," Benjamin said.

"Come in, come in, don't stand in a hallway. Goyim stand in hallways. Jews come in."

Benjamin and Paul came into the apartment and Grandma Gelfinbaum shut the door behind them. "Hello, it's nice you came to visit, Benjamin. Such a good boy. And you're Paul."

"Nice to meet you," Paul said.

"You want some salmon? Borscht? I've got leftover boiled chicken. You want some leftover boiled chicken?"

"No, we just came to say hi," Benjamin said quickly.

"Maybe your friend wants something to eat. Do you want something to eat, Paul? A nice piece of whitefish, some cholla?"

"No thanks," Paul said politely.

"Should we say hi to Grandpa before we go?" Benjamin asked.

"Look at him, he sits in the chair and watches Gene Autrey. What kind of a Jew is that? I tell you, it's enough to make a person have diarrhea." She turned her large body

161

toward the other room. "Hey, get up off the chair, you meshuga, and say hello to Benjamin and his friend."

They could hear Grandpa Gelfinbaum mumbling something, and they could hear him getting up off the chair. He came into the room. He was wearing wrinkled slacks and a white shirt. "I'm missing the commercial." He turned to Benjamin and said, "Why are you here?"

"We're going to POP, so I thought we should say hello," Benjamin said.

"POP," Grandpa Gelfinbaum said with disgust, as if just saying the letters left the taste of bile in his mouth. "And who is this?"

"This is my friend Paul."

Grandpa Gelfinbaum looked at Paul and said, "He's portly, isn't he?"

Paul started laughing, and that started Benjamin laughing.

Grandma Gelfinbaum looked at her husband and said, "That's nice, calling a person you just met portly. Go back in the other room, you shouldn't be allowed around other people."

"What did I say? I said he was portly. He's not portly? I know a portly person when I see one."

Paul was biting his lip, really trying to not laugh which, of course, just made him laugh more.

"Why are they laughing?" Grandpa Gelfinbaum asked.

"Because they can't believe anyone could be such a horse's tuchus, that's why."

Grandma Gelfinbaum turned back to the boys and said, "Sit, you'll have a macaroon, then you'll go."

Benjamin and Paul went to the table and sat down, while Grandma Gelfinbaum went to the kitchen to get the macaroons, which were in a jar on the old-fashioned stove. She brought the jar to the table and set it down. "Do you want some milk? Tea?"

They both shook their heads "no". She served them each a big macaroon. Grandpa Gelfinbaum sauntered over to the table. "What am I, chopped liver? You don't offer me a macaroon?"

"Go watch Gene Autrey. You smell like herring, you're disgusting."

Of course, rather than do what Grandma Gelfinbaum told him to, Grandpa Gelfinbaum sat down at the table and took a macaroon out of the jar. Just before he ate it in one gulp, he said, "What is it, fish?"

That was it. Paul, who was in the middle of swallowing, practically choked on his macaroon, he was laughing so hard. Grandpa Gelfinbaum looked at Paul, then at Benjamin, who was also laughing like a hyena. "Who am I, Georgie Jessel? Why do they keep laughing?"

"Sha, already," Grandma Gelfinbaum said. "They're laughing because you're a meshuganah old man."

Grandpa Gelfinbaum got up from the table, red-faced. "I don't have to listen to you. I'm going to make a stool." And with that, Grandpa Gelfinbaum went off into the bathroom.

Benjamin and Paul escaped from the apartment and spent the next few hours running around POP going on as many rides as possible. Of course, they did the Flight to Mars several times, the Ocean Skyway, the Magic Carpet, the House of Mirrors and they even found time for a game or two of Skeeball in the Penny Arcade. Paul tried to get Benjamin to go on the roller coaster but Benjamin wasn't having any of it, so Paul went by himself while Benjamin watched.

Before they caught the bus home, they stopped at the magic shop and Benjamin introduced Paul to Mr. Szymond, who showed them some of the latest tricks he'd gotten in.

*   *   *

And so it went; the two friends were inseparable. Paul became part of Benjamin's routine—the trips to Leo's for soda pop and pickles, the movies every week, watching *The Twilight Zone* and hanging out together at school whenever they could—and Benjamin became a regular fixture at the Daley house, where he did indeed learn to do the Limbo and the Twist.

They were like Abbott and Costello, and the kids at school began to laugh at their antics and their sayings. Benjamin, thanks in part to Paul, was now totally comfortable at Louis Pasteur. Butch Polsky had moved on and was tormenting other kids. The A7 was proving much easier for Benjamin and he liked most of his teachers. His after-school visits with Mr. Williamson continued and he was introduced to yet more wonderful music, not only classical, but the joys of jazz, too. You could create whole different sets of mind pictures with jazz and there was nowhere that your imagination couldn't run to. He heard Errol Garner play *Misty*, he heard Stan Getz and the Dave Brubeck Quartet and, best of all, he heard George Shearing play a wonderful song called *A Tune for Humming*, just piano and no other instruments—and that tune had Benjamin humming for a month (of course, he got the album it was from).

* * *

Somehow it was already May, and in a few weeks Benjamin would finish the A7 and summer vacation would start. He couldn't wait—there were so many things to do, so many movies to see, so many television shows to watch—a whole summer ahead—with the team of Kritzer and Daley doing nothing but what they felt like doing.

CHAPTER THREE

Death of Two Salesmen

Benjamin needed money. That is, he needed money if he was going to keep on buying record albums, going to the movies (and paying for Paul a lot of the time), and doing everything else he wanted to do. His allowance, while generous, wasn't nearly enough, and Minnie was getting tired of laying out money for everything that happened to catch Benjamin's eye, which was pretty much everything, and Benjamin was getting tired of having to do the chores which were the price of Minnie laying out money.

Funnily, an acquaintance of Paul's mother who employed young kids to sell subscriptions door-to-door for home and garden-type magazines had asked if Paul would be interested in trying his luck, and Paul, in turn, asked Benjamin if he'd like to try his luck, too. Benjamin thought that would be an easy way to make some extra cash so he said yes, even though it meant spending four hours of his Sunday doing it. After all, how hard could it be selling subscriptions door-to-door, especially with such a winning personality as his very own winning personality?

Benjamin told Minnie and Ernie about it, and they thought it would be a good thing for Benjamin to work and earn his own money.

And so, the following Sunday, bright and early, Frank, the magazine man, picked Benjamin and Paul up and drove them to Beverly Hills, which is where they were to attempt their magazine sales. There were two other kids in the car, Mel and Harlan, both twelve and both old hands at magazine subscription selling. They got dropped off first, near Olympic and Palm. Frank then drove a little further west and parked. He went over what he called the sales spiel (Benjamin loved that word immediately—spiel—it was almost like a spelled-backwards word only it wasn't spelled backwards).

Since they were all sitting in a not-huge 1954 Plymouth, Benjamin could barely stand the rather disgusting aroma of Frank the magazine man's breath, which smelled like he'd eaten several dead rats. The smell was probably due to the fact that Frank the magazine man's teeth had seen better days—several of them were brown and rotted, and there were occasional spaces where there weren't any teeth at all. He also had a very pungent body odor, extremely greasy black hair and he had a strange habit of winding up for a belch but never quite delivering it. Of course, it didn't help that Frank, the magazine man, had all the windows in the 1954 Plymouth rolled up, thereby making the stench even worse.

He gave the boys magazine samples and order forms and an envelope in which to put their takings. Paul got out where they were parked to work the neighborhood of Olympic up to Wilshire, and a five-block radius to the west (Frank, the magazine man, thought Beverly Hills was prime subscription territory, because everyone was rich and, rather than be bothered on a Sunday, they'd simply take the subscription to be rid of the bothersome interruption— especially when the subscription was offered by a nice, clean-cut American boy). He drove Benjamin five blocks further west, to Roxbury, and dropped him off there (just in the nick of time, because if Benjamin had spent one more minute in that 1954 Plymouth inhaling the fumes of Frank, the magazine man, he would have vomited right there on the ground or, at the very least, on the yellowing stained upholstery of the back seat.

It was eleven o'clock when Benjamin started working the neighborhood. The boys were all to meet back at three o'clock at Roxbury and Olympic. The first problem was that the temperature was already well into the high nineties and there was no breeze at all, just hot stultifying air. The second problem was that after doing the spiel at ten houses, no one seemed interested in taking a subscription from a smiling American boy with a winning personality. In fact, a couple of people had seemed downright hostile and had slammed the door in Benjamin's smiling face.

By noon he was sweating (which was very unusual for Benjamin, who normally never sweated) and already tired of doing the spiel. He still had had no success whatsoever and was beginning to doubt that he would. Maybe, he thought, it was just the block he was on, so he walked a block west and tried another.

The first two houses were a bust. The third house he tried was one of those old but still beautiful Spanish-style homes which were so popular in Los Angeles. As Benjamin went up the path, he saw that the walkway was lined with multi-colored roses (the official flower of Kritzerland)—red, pink, yellow—roses that were all abloom and bursting with color and fragrance. As Benjamin passed them, he stuck his nose close so he could breathe in that amazing scent. He got to the front door and knocked. He could hear the sound of a vacuum cleaner coming from somewhere in the house. After a minute, Benjamin rang the doorbell. He heard the vacuum cleaner shut off, and then a moment later he could hear footsteps coming to the door.

The door opened and Benjamin was greeted by a beautiful lady dressed in orange pants, a white and blue pullover top and sandals. She looked at Benjamin, smiled, and said, "Yes?"

"Hello, my name is Benjamin Kritzer and I'm here to offer you a special deal on these wonderful magazines. If you purchase a subscription today you will save fifty-percent off the store price. Would you like to purchase one?"

The beautiful lady laughed and her laugh suddenly made the day bearable. She looked at Benjamin and said, "You look quite hot. Would you like to come in and have a glass of lemonade? I've just made some and it's really good."

Benjamin nodded his head "yes" and the lady ushered him into the house.

"Come in and sit. I'll get the lemonade."

She led Benjamin to the living room, which had high ceilings, tapestries with intricate and beautiful designs hanging on two of the walls, and furnishings which were simple but elegant. "I'll be right back," the beautiful lady said and she went off to wherever the lemonade was.

Benjamin had noticed that the beautiful lady had an accent, a French accent he surmised, even though she spoke excellent English. Sunlight streamed through the large windows leaving odd patterns on the wood floor. Hanging above the fireplace was a painting of the beautiful lady when she was younger and even more beautiful.

She came back into the living room with two tall glasses of lemonade sitting on a tray. She gave one to Benjamin and took the other herself, and then sat down next to Benjamin on the cream-colored sofa. "Now," she said, in her lilting accent, "tell me about these magazines."

Benjamin showed her the sample copies and she paged through them quite earnestly. "These look quite nice. Which one would you recommend?" she asked. Benjamin didn't have a clue, so he just pointed to the one called *Garden World.* "Isn't that funny, that's the one I was thinking, too," the beautiful lady said. "So, what do you make if I should take a subscription to this magazine?"

"Fifty cents," Benjamin replied.

"And how many subscriptions have you sold so far?"

"None."

The beautiful lady smiled at Benjamin. "Well, we can't have that, can we, Benjamin? So, I will take a subscription to *Garden World*, how's that?"

"That is great," said Benjamin, with a large smile on his face. The beautiful lady lifted her glass of lemonade in a toast and she and Benjamin clinked the glasses together. He practically downed the contents of the glass in one big gulp—it was wonderful-tasting, refreshing and tart and a perfect antidote to the heat. She filled out the subscription form and handed him the money. "There, now you've made a sale."

Benjamin finished the last bit of his lemonade, and then pointed at the picture above the fireplace. "Is that you?" he asked.

"Yes, that's me, just before I came to this country to be an actress. I was twenty when that was painted."

"You're an actress?" Benjamin asked with some amazement.

"Well, there was always some question about how *good* an actress, but yes, I did quite a few films." She threw her head back and laughed. "But you know, Benjamin, they don't care about you here if you're not a young actress, and I'm thirty-five and over-the-hill I guess, since I don't work very much anymore. Still, I've had fun and that's what life is about, isn't it?"

"What's your name?" Benjamin asked.

"Corinne Calvet," the beautiful lady said, and the name sounded magical with her accent.

"Well, Benjamin, I have to get back to cleaning." She got up, as did Benjamin, and she walked him to the door. "You have brightened my Sunday, Benjamin, and I will think of you every time a new issue of *Garden World* arrives."

She put her hand out and Benjamin shook it. It was soft as velvet and he didn't want to let go of it. She smiled, waved "goodbye" and closed the door.

He worked the rest of the neighborhood and at 2:45 he headed back to Olympic and Roxbury without having made one additional sale. He was hot, tired, and sweaty, but he'd met Corinne Calvet and that had made the whole day worthwhile.

When he got back to the car, Mel and Harlan were already in the back seat and Paul was sitting on the curb, breathing heavily, face red as a beet.

"How'd you do?" Paul asked.

"I sold one subscription, to an actress, a beautiful actress. Corinne Calvet. How'd you do?"

"Not one. Four hours and not one bite. I quit."

"Me, too," said Benjamin.

They both got in the front seat and Benjamin handed Frank, the magazine man, the money for Corinne Calvet's subscription. Frank gave Benjamin his fifty-cent commission and started the car. He turned to Benjamin and Paul and said, "Don't worry, you'll get used to it, it gets easier the more you do it." He gunned the motor and began the drive back.

Frank, the magazine man, dropped Benjamin and Paul at Benjamin's house and as they got out of the hot, disgusting-smelling car, they informed him that they were quitting. He tried to talk them into giving it one more shot, but to no avail. Even if they'd had great success, neither Benjamin nor Paul ever wanted to set foot in that smelly 1954 Plymouth again, as long as they lived.

* * *

The school semester ended and Benjamin's report card wasn't too bad—mostly C's and B's, all S's and E's in cooperation and work habits. He did get an AEE in Music Appreciation, and that grade meant more to him than all the grades he'd ever gotten.

*   *   *

The first week of summer, Benjamin got two pieces of rather shocking news: The first piece of shocking news was that Paul would be leaving in three weeks to go to summer camp. As if that weren't bad enough, there was the second piece of shocking news: Benjamin was also leaving—Minnie and Ernie were going to Florida and Benjamin would be going on a trip to St. Louis for a week with one of Ernie's waitresses, Bonnie, her son, Ronny, and Bonnie's new husband, Harry.

CHAPTER FOUR

Benjamin Goes to St. Louis

Benjamin and Paul got in as much time as they could before Paul left for camp. They went to the movies (they saw *The Bellboy*, *The Lost World*, *Portrait in Black*, and, best of all, *Hercules Unchained*), they played miniature golf, they ate pizza at Big Town Market, they watched the new A&P market being built, and they had their weekly *Twilight Zone* ritual (their current favorite was an especially creepy episode about mannequins in a department store). As it turned out, Paul would only be gone for a month, and since Benjamin would be gone for a week, he'd only have three weeks without his friend.

Benjamin didn't like the thought of going to St. Louis. He had several reasons. One, he'd never been away from home before and he didn't like the thought of being in a strange place for a week. Two, he was going to be in a strange place with strangers. Oh, he'd known Bonnie for a year, ever since she'd come to work at the Erro, and he'd even gone to the Wiltern with her son, Ronny (who was Benjamin's age), and he'd even met her new husband, Harry, whom Benjamin didn't like one bit. Harry was a tough customer, a liquor salesman (he sold to all of Ernie's establishments), mostly bald, with a volatile temper.

Once, in the alley behind the Erro, Benjamin had seen Harry get into a fight with another man because the other man had winked at Bonnie. There they were, two grown men, rolling around on the ground hitting each other. It wasn't like on television, no, not like that at all. They were red-faced and grunting and there was real blood coming out of real Harry's bald head, and for all Benjamin knew the two fighting men might have killed each other had Bonnie not put a stop to it (she was a tough customer, too) by running into the Erro, getting a skillet, and then clobbering the winking man on the head with it.

Benjamin had even spent the night once at Bonnie's and all he remembered about it was that Ronny kept asking if he could get into bed and sleep next to him. It was a strange thing to ask, Benjamin thought, but since Benjamin was highly claustrophobic in tight places, there was no way anyone was sleeping in the same bed as him. And besides who wanted to sleep with another person in the bed?

* * *

Paul left for camp on a Monday. Benjamin drove with Paul and his mother to the place where the bus was waiting to take Paul to camp. Once there, they said goodbye to each other and Paul said he couldn't wait to get back because there was so much to do. Paul and his mother hugged and kissed goodbye, and then Paul got on the bus and was driven away to some God-forsaken camp place.

Benjamin was set to leave a few days later and he was getting quite nervous about it. It would be his first trip and his first time on an airplane. However, he knew all about airplanes because he'd seen *The High and the Mighty*. Sure, John Wayne had flown that plane to safety after it looked like it was going to crash, but Benjamin doubted that John Wayne was going to be his pilot and therefore was very apprehensive about riding on an airplane. Minnie had also warned him that people threw up on airplanes and that if Benjamin had the urge to do so, there was a "vomit bag" located in the seat pocket (whatever that was). Just the thought of a "vomit bag" made Benjamin want to vomit.

"Do I really have to go?" Benjamin asked, the day before the trip.

"Is the Pope Catholic?" Minnie replied.

"The Pope? Who's the Pope?"

"Who's the Pope? The Pope, that's who's the Pope."

"Why are you asking if he's Catholic?"

"I'm not asking. He *is* Catholic. It's just a saying—you know, is the Pope Catholic."

"But if you know the Pope is Catholic why are you asking if the Pope is Catholic?"

"Benjamin, go take a long walk off a short pier, will you? You'll have fun in St. Louis. You've never been anywhere in your whole life, Benjamin. It will be good for you."

"But I don't want to go."

"Tough. You're going and you'll have fun. Period."

To make him feel better, she gave Benjamin some money to buy a book so he'd have something to read on the airplane and while he was in St. Louis. They went to the Daylight Market and Benjamin went to the paperback book rack and spun it around until something caught his eye. It was a book called *Psycho* by someone named Robert Bloch. It had a photo of a screaming lady on the cover and the front of the book said it was about to be a major motion picture from Alfred Hitchcock. That did the trick—Alfred Hitchcock was Benjamin's favorite, so if he was making a movie from the book, the book had to be great. He bought it immediately. When he rejoined Minnie in the car she asked what he'd gotten. He pulled the book out of the bag and showed it to her.

"*Psycho?*" she said, with a sneer in her voice. "This is the kind of book you buy? *Psycho?*"

"It's going to be an Alfred Hitchcock movie. This way I'll read it and then know what the movie is about when I see it. Besides, it sounds like a really good book, really scary."

"It sounds like dreck. Whatever happened to nice books, like The Hardy Boys?"

The night before the trip, Minnie packed a suitcase for Benjamin. She put enough clothes in it to last him the week. Jeffrey was also packing to stay at a friend's house until Minnie and Ernie's return four days later. That night, Jeffrey regaled Benjamin with stories of airplanes that had crashed into the ground. Benjamin barely slept the entire night.

The following morning, Bonnie, Ronny and Harry arrived to pick Benjamin up. Ernie loaded the suitcase into the already crowded trunk and Minnie nudged the reluctant Benjamin into the back seat next to Ronny.

"Have fun, Benjamin. We'll see you when you get back," Minnie said.

That was it. No hugs, no kisses, no nothing. Here Benjamin was about to go off on an airplane that might crash to the ground and his Martian parents couldn't even offer a hug or a kiss like normal parents. Paul and his mother had hugged and kissed before Paul had gone off to some God-forsaken camp place. It seemed like such a nice thing to do.

Harry pulled the car, a red 1958 Chevrolet, away from the curb. Minnie and Ernie were already headed back into the house. Harry turned left on 18th and headed over to La Cienega, where he turned right. Ronny was sitting next to Benjamin with his lower lip stuck out, pouting. Bonnie turned her head around, looked at Ronny and said, "Oh, stop bein' so crabby, Mr. Crabapple." She looked over at Benjamin and said, "Mr. Crabby over there had a little temper tantrum this morning, didn't you Mr. Crabby?" Ronny's lower lip protruded another inch and he sat there with his arms crossed, not saying a word, for the entire trip to the airport.

As they drove south, they passed the oil derricks which lined La Cienega. Benjamin stared out the window, watching them pump, up and down and around, up and down and around. Bonnie turned toward the back seat again and said, "We're gonna have a great time, Benjamin. My sister got tickets for all of us to go to the Muny. That's a big theater where they do musicals. It's outdoors. I used to go there all the time."

Benjamin nodded and smiled. Bonnie looked over at Ronny and said, "Are you going to sit there like a bump on a log the whole time?" Since Ronny had no answer, apparently he was going to do just that.

They arrived at Los Angeles International Airport (Benjamin had been to the airport once, to pick up his Uncle Rube when he'd come in from Brooklyn one year). Harry checked the bags and they all went into the terminal. Bonnie had her arm around Ronny, and he kept trying to shrug it off. They stood in line for a while, while Bonnie and Harry did something with their tickets at the counter. After that, they all went to the boarding gate.

An hour later they boarded the TWA airplane. Their seats were way in the back and were quite tiny and uncomfortable. There were three seats across: Ronny took the window seat, Benjamin was in the middle and Bonnie was on the aisle. Harry sat across from her in the first seat in the middle row. Benjamin's knee was going up and down like a jackhammer. He saw there was a pocket in the seat in front of him (that must have been the seat pocket Minnie had spoken of) and he saw the vomit bag sticking out of it. He pulled it out and looked at it. There were instructions on the front, the gist of which were that if you were going to vomit you simply opened the bag and deposited your vomit directly within.

He put the bag back in the pocket and sat there, waiting for the plane to take off. He had his new book, *Psycho*, on his lap and Bonnie had fastened his seatbelt for him because he simply could not figure it out. A stewardess came out and demonstrated the airplane safety precautions. Benjamin hoped there wouldn't be any problems because there was no way on earth he would ever be able to figure out how to put the oxygen mask on.

Finally, the airplane doors were shut and the engines were turned on. It was quite loud and Benjamin looked out the window to see the big propellers whirling maniacally. The blades were spinning so fast that they were barely perceptible, and for some reason it reminded Benjamin of the Chop-o-Matic. The plane taxied onto the runway and then began to move more swiftly. Benjamin's hands gripped the armrest tightly, so tightly that his arms hurt. The plane gained speed and, with a bump, was suddenly off the ground.

It wasn't so bad after all. Benjamin had no urge to vomit into the vomit bag, and as he looked out the window (which was difficult given that Ronny's large head was in the way), he could see the plane rising higher and higher and the city getting smaller and smaller. He wondered where his house was, wondered if he could see it from the airplane. Of course, this was how *The High and the Mighty* had started; everything was perfectly fine and then all hell had broken loose. But, maybe that was just how it happened in the movies. After all, thousands of people flew every day with no problems. He looked over at Ronny who'd already fallen asleep, his head bobbing up and down like an apple in water. Bonnie and Harry were conversing across the aisle, so Benjamin opened *Psycho* and began reading it.

Forty-five minutes later he got to the end of Chapter Three. A nice lady, Mary Crane, had resolved to return some money she'd taken, and she had just gotten into the shower in a motel run by a creepy guy named Norman Bates, who had a mean mother. Suddenly, the curtains parted and someone was there—a crazy old woman with a butcher knife. Benjamin's eyes widened like saucers as he read the last few lines:

"It was the same knife that, a moment later, cut off her scream. And her head."

This was better than *The Twilight Zone*. This was supremely creepy, the creepiest thing Benjamin had ever read. He couldn't wait to tell Paul about it. He couldn't wait to see the movie. He couldn't wait to get to Chapter Four. By the time he reached St. Louis, he'd gotten three-quarters of the way through the book and had totally forgotten he was even on an airplane.

* * *

They arrived at Bonnie's sister's house by early evening. Benjamin and Ronny would be staying in the downstairs den, on cots. Bonnie's sister, Linda, a tired-looking woman who always had a cigarette dangling from her mouth, had two kids of her own, boys, named Bradley and Thomas. They both had scraggly blonde hair and were thin as rails. From the moment Benjamin met them, Bradley and Thomas never stopped braying and whining and running around the house like wildly spinning dreidls (not that these people would have a clue what a dreidl was—these people were Baptists and proud of it). Linda's husband was a perpetually red-faced man named Lester who had a huge beer belly that hung precariously over his pants like a giant-sized mound of quivering Jell-O.

Benjamin found the den very interesting. First of all, there was a slot machine. There was money in the tray to

181

play with and Benjamin immediately became obsessed with the slot machine. Every time he'd pull the arm down, he'd say "Franklin" like the slot machine had in that episode of *The Twilight Zone*. There was a large bar with a huge electric Bush Bavarian beer sign, the colorful letters sitting atop a river that actually seemed to be flowing. Benjamin was not too keen on the bathroom, which he'd checked out immediately. It looked like it had been assembled from a kit, and the shower stall was grimy and had weird-looking shiny stuff on the floor. Later, he was told that the weird-looking shiny stuff was silverfish and that gave him the willies. He didn't want to shower where there was something called silverfish, but what could he do; he had no choice unless he wanted to go dirty. The cots were extremely lumpy and uncomfortable and, all in all, he couldn't wait for the week to be over.

* * *

During the week, everyone went sightseeing. All Benjamin wanted to do was finish reading *Psycho*, but they had non-stop plans for every day, and Benjamin got very little time to himself.

They went to the zoo in Forest Park. Benjamin had never been to a zoo before and as far as he was concerned it would be fine if he never went to a zoo again as long as he lived. The animals were all right, but the whole place smelled of their bathroom activities and it was very hot and tiring and Bradley and Thomas kept throwing things at the animals and taunting them. Ronny pouted the whole time because Bonnie wouldn't buy him a corn dog.

They ate at Stan Musial's, a steak house not unlike
Ernie's but not nearly as good, in Benjamin's humble
opinion. Furthermore, there was no sign of Stan the Man
himself. Benjamin remembered always choosing Stan the
Man Musial when he and Jeffrey played their baseball board
game, and here Benjamin was in Stan the Man's restaurant
and Stan the Man couldn't even be bothered to show up.
As usual, Bradley and Thomas spent most of the evening
under the table kicking everyone and scrambling about, and
Ronny pouted over some injustice or other. Linda smoked
endlessly, Lester drank beer endlessly, and Bonnie and
Harry, the newlyweds, argued endlessly.

They went on the Admiral, a riverboat with three levels,
which cruised up and down the Mississippi River. That was
fun for about ten minutes. Unfortunately, they were on the
boat for an hour. The whole time, Bradley would whine,
"I'm thirsty, I'm hungry, I have to pee" and Thomas would
whine, "I'm itchy, I have to *poo*." And Harry would pick on
Bonnie and Bonnie would razz him right back, and Ronny,
as always, sulked.

At one home-cooked dinner, Lester offered all the kids
their own bottle of Bush Bavarian beer. "It'll put hair on
your chest," he said to Benjamin. Lester handed each of
the kids an ice-cold bottle—his face was so red Benjamin
thought it might explode at any minute. Bradley and
Thomas were old hands at beer drinking, and they gulped
theirs down quickly and messily. "Can I have another
one?" Bradley brayed. "Me, too, me too," Thomas whined.
Ronny sipped at his sullenly.

"Go on, Benjamin, you'll like it," Lester said. "Nothin'
like a cold Bush to wash away your troubles."

Benjamin didn't think he had any troubles to wash away, and he didn't know that he wanted hair on his chest. But he tried, oh, yes, he tried—the bottle was ice-cold and it looked just like a soda pop, but when he took a slug he couldn't believe how foul-tasting it was and he nearly spit it out right there on the dining room table. The others saw the look on his face and laughed. "Kinda tastes like horse piss, doesn't it, but you get used to it," Linda said. "Horse piss, horse piss," Bradley cackled. "Horse *poo*, horse *poo*," Thomas chimed in, and everyone laughed and laughed and guzzled their beer; everyone, that is, except Benjamin, who sat there thinking he was in the middle of some horrible nightmare.

Every night, Ronny would wander over to Benjamin's cot and try to get in bed with him. Ronny was like a pesky dog—the more you said "go away" the more persistent he became. Benjamin would nicely say "there's no room" and then Ronny would try to lie down anyway, and Benjamin would have to push him off the bed onto the floor, where Ronny would lie and sulk before going back to his own cot. Benjamin couldn't wait to be back in his own house, in his own room, in his own bed, away from this unending madness.

On the night before their departure, the entire group went to the Muny to see a show called *Rosalie*. The Muny was a huge outdoor theater and Benjamin was very impressed with how many seats there were; there were seats as far as the eye could see. Their seats were quite far up and the stage looked tiny from where they were.

The show began and Benjamin sat there with his mouth open. The orchestra sounded wonderful, the stage was beautifully lit, the scenery looked nice and it was all very magical.   The whole theater was full, and everyone applauded at the end of each song. He couldn't really even follow the story, but every time they sang he loved it. He especially liked the title song, *Rosalie*. It had a lovely melody and it embedded itself into Benjamin's head and he could not get that tune to go away.

> *Rosalie, my darling*
> *Rosalie, my love*

He sang it to himself over and over: at intermission, on the ride home, as he was packing his suitcase, as he was shoving Ronny off his cot, as he played his final few turns on the slot machine, and as he finally, mercifully, bid farewell to Linda, Lester, Bradley and Thomas.

He sang it to himself on the way to the airport, at the gate waiting to board the plane, and in his seat while they waited to take off.

Before he started to read the last of *Psycho*, Benjamin had to thumb through the book to remind himself of where he'd left off. The book had a surprise ending that so caught Benjamin off-guard that he went back and reread whole chapters just to make sure he understood it.

Benjamin had survived (barely) his first trip away from home and his first trip on an airplane. He hadn't used the vomit bag, he'd seen his first live musical show (*Rosalie, my darling, Rosalie my love*), he'd played a real slot machine and he'd finished reading *Psycho*. He couldn't wait to see the movie and hoped it would be out soon. When Bonnie, Ronny and Harry dropped him at home, his parents acted as if he'd never even been gone.

CHAPTER FIVE

Sneak Previews, and
The 16mm Movie Camera

Benjamin wouldn't stop singing the title song from *Rosalie* and it was driving Minnie crazy. It was worse than *I Guess Things Happen That Way* because Benjamin tried to emulate the semi-operatic voice of the man who sang it in the show. He'd walk around the house and he'd sing it and he'd sing it and then he'd sing it some more.

"Rosalie, my darling, Rosalie, my love"

It was like fingernails on a blackboard to Minnie, and she finally couldn't stand it anymore.

"Benjamin," she said, "will you drop dead with that song already? Rosalie, Rosalie, Rosalie, it's from hunger."

"Actually, it's from *Rosalie*. I saw it in St. Louis. You remember I went to St. Louis, don't you?"

"What am I, an idiot? Of course I know you went to St. Louis. What has that got to do with the price of tomatoes?"

Benjamin honestly didn't know what it had to do with the price of tomatoes so instead of replying he sang, "Rosalie, my darling, Rosalie my love."

Minnie's teeth began moving around in her mouth, clattering like toy wind-up teeth. "Stop it this minute. You have a terrible voice and I don't want to hear it anymore."

Benjamin stopped. "I have a terrible voice?"

"Yes, you have a terrible voice—you think you have a good voice? You think what's coming out of your mouth is pleasant?"

Benjamin didn't think he had a terrible voice, especially when he sang in the shower. He thought he sounded like Ricky Nelson or Paul Anka or Frankie Avalon. He turned to his mother. "Why do I have a terrible voice?"

"Why. How do I know why? Frank Sinatra you're not."

"What has that got to do with the price of tomatoes?" Benjamin asked.

"Can't you go play in traffic? Can't you go in your room and listen to your record player? I can't wait until your friend is back from camp. Maybe then I can have some peace and quiet. In fact, let me put it to you this way—we were going to take you to the Village tonight—there's a sneak preview. But if you sing that song once more, you will be staying home."

Since Benjamin didn't want to miss a sneak preview he immediately went outside and played in the yard where he, of course, sang *Rosalie*.

Benjamin loved sneak previews. He loved seeing movies before anyone else saw them. Some sneak previews were

187

shown *months* before the movie would actually come out, and he felt like he was "in the know" because he saw it so far in advance. Sometimes the stars of the movie were at the sneak preview, so that was exciting, too.

The first sneak preview he'd seen was in 1954 (he remembered it as if it were yesterday). Minnie and Ernie had bundled Benjamin and Jeffrey into the car and they'd gone to the Baldwin Theater. Benjamin had been wearing jeans, his pajama top and a pair of slippers. The sneak preview was a science fiction movie called *Target Earth*. It was a strange movie about four people in a totally deserted town, and Benjamin was enjoying it. That is, he was enjoying it until the hideously scary robot made its first appearance. That frightened young Benjamin Kritzer so much that he'd scrambled up the aisle and out of the theater faster than a speeding bullet (since then, only a handful of movies had ever scared him sufficiently to send him scurrying up the aisle). On his way out the front door he ran right through a big batch of shrubbery and ivy in front of the theater. When he got out of the ivy his right slipper was missing. Eventually, he got up the nerve to go back into the theater and he watched the rest of the film, ready to bolt at any minute if something scary happened. When the movie was over, Minnie had noticed Benjamin was missing his right slipper. He told her that it had come off while he was in the ivy. She and Ernie had searched for ten minutes but could not find the slipper. It had simply disappeared off the face of the earth.

His second sneak preview was the following year, when he saw *The Tender Trap* at the Village Theater, in glorious Cinemascope and Stereophonic Sound. Benjamin never forgot the opening of the film with Frank Sinatra (who

Benjamin was not) walking along against a huge blue sky singing the title song. After that, the Kritzers went regularly to sneak previews—some good, some bad, but Benjamin didn't care one way or the other because he was "in the know".

That night, Minnie, Ernie, and Benjamin headed off to Westwood. They ate at the Apple Pan, where Benjamin had his favorite, the Hickory Burger. Oh, how he loved the Hickory Burger, not to mention the apple pie. The restaurant itself reminded him of Kentucky Boys—just a counter, no booths—the difference being that the Apple Pan was always crowded and people had to invariably stand and wait for the diners at the counter to leave.

They got to the theater at seven-thirty and waited until the previous show let out. They found seats (Benjamin, as usual, moved down to the tenth row, where his aisle seat was happily available). Intermission lasted about fifteen minutes, and then they showed a newsreel, a cartoon (a Mr. Magoo, which Benjamin always enjoyed), and coming attractions. Then the curtains closed, and as they were closing Benjamin could see the black masking of the screen expanding, so he knew the movie was going to be in Cinemascope. The 20th Century Fox logo came on as the curtains reopened. This was followed by sprightly music, which Benjamin was taken with immediately. The titles were cute and fun—the film was called *High Time*, and it starred Bing Crosby and other people Benjamin hadn't heard of.

Well, he loved it. The film got howls of laughter and no one howled harder than Benjamin Kritzer. He couldn't wait for it to come out so he could see it several more times. He met Minnie and Ernie in the lobby and, as they walked out of the theater, Benjamin could see there was a large crowd of people gathered near the box office, gawking and chattering excitedly. The three Kritzers got closer to the crowd, and standing there, next to the box office, was Bing Crosby himself, smiling and greeting people and waving to the crowd. Near him was the pretty girl from the film, Tuesday Weld. Everyone was saying how much they loved the movie and how big a hit it was going to be. It was all very exciting to see movie stars in person, even for Minnie and Ernie who were gawking and chattering like everyone else. Benjamin was humming the theme constantly in the days following the preview, and for Minnie it was blessed relief from *Rosalie*.

A few weeks later, the three of them went to another sneak preview, this one at the Wilshire. The main feature was a movie called *Let's Make Love*, with Marilyn Monroe. They arrived towards the end of *Let's Make Love* and saw the last half-hour of it. Benjamin hated that, hated coming in late to a movie. He had no idea what was going on and just sat there totally confused. He did think Marilyn Monroe was quite pretty, though. The theater was jammed and Benjamin had to content himself with not only not having his tenth-row aisle seat but also with sitting next to his parents. There was a brief intermission (Ernie went out and got everyone buttered popcorn—extra butter for Benjamin—and Cokes). He got back just as the coming attractions were starting. Then the sneak preview began and as soon as the audience found out what they were seeing, there was a groan of disappointment. It was a foreign movie, dubbed in English, called *Come Dance with Me*, and it starred Brigitte Bardot.

Ernie perked right up—he thought Brigitte Bardot was a knockout. Minnie sat there shaking her head back and forth as if that would somehow make the movie go away. Benjamin had already seen Brigitte Bardot in a movie, *La Parisienne*, which had played at the Stadium, and he thought she, like Marilyn Monroe, was beautiful, so he didn't mind the movie at all, even though it wasn't very funny (he was quite certain it was supposed to be funny, because everyone was running around crazily and that usually meant something was funny).

About forty minutes into the film, Brigitte Bardot was wearing an extremely tiny nightie which barely covered her, and she was lying on a bed with a man. She and the man were being playful and kissing. Ernie, unlike most times at the movies, was wide awake and glued to the screen, which seemed to annoy Minnie even more than if he'd been snoring as usual. She kept shaking her head back and forth, which Benjamin found very distracting. Suddenly, the man was undoing the little strap that held the little nightie that barely covered Brigitte Bardot, and as he lowered it, just before you could actually see anything, he put his actual hand right on top of her actual breast. Minnie took one look at that and was on her feet stepping in front of Benjamin and grabbing his arm, literally yanking him out of his seat and dragging him up the aisle while saying, "That's filthy. You are not seeing that." When she got him into the lobby, she realized that Ernie hadn't followed them. She told Benjamin to wait there and she went back into the theater.

Benjamin opened the door and stood at the top of the aisle, but the scene with Brigitte and the man was already over. The scene in the actual movie theater was just beginning, however, with Minnie stomping her way down the aisle. It was so dark she couldn't find the row that they'd been sitting in, and she just kept pacing up and down trying to find Ernie. She stopped where she thought he was and whispered loudly, "Ernie! Ernie! Ernie!" Apparently there were no Ernies in that row, so she moved down the aisle and started again. "Ernie! Ernie! Ernie!" People were beginning to shush her, and one annoyed patron said, "Will you shut up?" She moved down a row or two and once again whispered loudly, "Ernie! Ernie! Ernie!" This time she'd found the right row because Ernie replied, "What?" in a disgruntled voice. "We're going," Minnie whispered, although Benjamin could hear it all the way at the top of the aisle. "Get up, we're leaving." Benjamin saw Ernie rise, and then he and Minnie were heading up the aisle. Benjamin scooted out the door and acted as if he'd been waiting in the lobby.

As they walked out of the theater, Ernie said, "What is the matter with you? I was enjoying the movie."

Minnie looked at him with disgust and said, "You were enjoying the movie. You think your twelve-year-old son should see a naked woman like that? It's filthy."

"Oh, please," Ernie said. "There are worse things than seeing a naked woman."

Minnie stopped dead in her tracks and wheeled around. "Like what?"

"I don't know," Ernie replied. "I'm sure there are worse things. He could steal a car."

"He could steal a car. You are such an idiot. He's twelve, what would he do with a car? The two of you will be the death of me yet."

Later that night, Ernie took Benjamin aside and told him to take everything his mother said and did with a grain of salt because she was having her "change of life". Benjamin didn't have a clue as to what that meant but whatever it was he hoped he would never have to go through it.

That was the last sneak preview the Kritzers attended together. From then on, Benjamin would go by himself.

*   *   *

Paul came back from camp and he and Benjamin picked right up where they'd left off. Benjamin told Paul all about *Psycho* and *Rosalie* and sang, "Rosalie, my darling, Rosalie my love" for him. He told him about *High Time* and he told him about the man who'd put his hand on Brigitte Bardot's actual breast and how his mother had dragged him up the aisle like a crazy person.

Paul told Benjamin all about camp—how uncomfortable the bunk beds had been, how he hated hiking, how his mother had come to visit and embarrassed him by doing the Twist in front of everyone, and, worst of all, how he'd awakened one morning to find his face covered in huge red bumps, the result of some hungry mosquito deciding that Paul's face was a perfect meal. All in all, he was thrilled to be home, and he and Benjamin celebrated by having a pickle and soda pop at Leo's and then a Fosters Freeze ice cream cone.

*   *   *

One late July morning, Benjamin was alone in the house, so he decided to go on one of his rummaging expeditions.

This time he went to the front hall closet. There were quite a few smaller boxes on a shelf, plus various coats on hangers (the same hangers that Minnie used to use on Benjamin—one of the reasons he rarely opened the front closet). He went through all the pockets of the various hanging coats and between all of them found sixty-three cents in small change.

Next, he got a chair from the dining room, brought it to the closet and climbed up on it so he could check out the boxes on the shelf. Two of them had hats, ugly hats with veils, which smelled of mothballs, which was only natural since there were moth balls in the boxes. Benjamin picked up one of the moth balls and wondered what the little white balls had to do with moths. The next box he opened had old photos in it, mostly of Minnie and Ernie when they'd first gotten married. There were some of the Gelfinbaums, some of Grandpa Kritzer, some of Jeffrey when he was a baby and, as usual, no photos of Benjamin save for one— he and Jeffrey sitting on some department store Santa's knee, with Benjamin looking at the Santa as if to say, "Who do you think you're fooling?"

But it was behind that box that Benjamin found the most interesting thing. And the most interesting thing he found was a Bell and Howell 16mm movie camera, along with a 16mm movie projector and what looked like three unused yellow boxes of Kodak 16mm film. Benjamin got them down, put the chair back in the dining room, and took the camera, projector, and film into his room.

The Bell and Howell 16mm movie camera was wonderfully intricate-looking. It had a sort of swivel thing with three different-sized lenses on it, and by turning the swivel thing the lenses would rotate. It had a viewfinder to look through and a wind-up switch on the side and was fairly heavy to hold. Benjamin looked through the viewfinder and could see a little square which showed him what the lens was seeing. As he rotated the swivel thing, the image got further away or closer. He wound the camera up and pressed the start button and it made a loud whirring noise as the wind-up switch went around and around. The projector was even more complicated-looking. Benjamin plugged it in and turned it on and it worked, projecting a shaft of light on the wall in a square shape, just like a movie in a theater.

He showed the camera to Paul when he came over at noon. They decided that since they had three rolls of film and a movie camera, they should make some movies. They went in the back yard and talked about what sort of movies they might make. Benjamin thought it would be fun to take the camera up to Hollywood to make their movies. Benjamin promised to write some ideas down, and they made a plan to go first thing in the morning.

That night, Benjamin cornered Ernie and showed him the Bell and Howell 16mm movie camera.

"Where did you find that?" Ernie asked. "I haven't seen that in years."

"It was in the hall closet. Can I use it?"

"Use it for what?"

"Paul and I want to make some movies."

"Oh, you do, do you? Well, you need film to do that."

Benjamin held up the three yellow boxes of Kodak film. Ernie looked at them and scratched the hair on the side of his head.

"Well, that's not very much film," he said. "I think each of those is five minutes or something. What kind of movies are you going to make?"

"I'm not sure yet."

"Well, you don't want to waste film, so you should write down exactly what you want to do, like a script."

"That's what I was going to do."

Benjamin went off to his room and spent the whole night planning what he and Paul would shoot the next day. He got some cardboard from his father's laundered shirts and, using his crayons, made up a series of title cards. He wrote down all his ideas on two pieces of lined notebook paper, and then called Paul and read them to him. Paul thought it sounded great. Benjamin finally went to bed at eleven, but he was so excited he couldn't sleep. He turned on the transistor radio and put in the earpiece. The song *The Twist* by Chubby Checker was just ending. The deejay came on and said that it had just reached number six on the charts. Paul's mother had been right—*The Twist* was going to be the number one song in the country. He twirled the dial aimlessly—he heard a bit of *Itsy Bitsy Teenie Weenie Yellow Polka Dot Bikini* and then Roy Orbison singing *Only the Lonely*, but all he could think about was the 16mm movie camera and going to Hollywood in the morning.

The morning finally arrived and he headed over to Paul's house, carrying the heavy camera in a shopping bag. They took the bus up to Hollywood and got off at Sunset and La Brea. They walked up La Brea and over to their first location, which was Grauman's Chinese. Benjamin had loaded the camera the night before (Ernie showed him how—it was quite simple once you got the hang of it) and so they were ready to shoot. It was a nice sunny day, a perfect day to make a movie. First Paul held one of the cardboard title cards in front of him. Benjamin wound the camera and made a brief shot of it—it said: KRITZER AND DALEY'S HOLLYWOOD ADVENTURES.

Then Paul held up the next title card and Benjamin shot that one. It said: THAT SINKING FEELING.

After that was done, Paul took his place by the famous footsteps in cement.

Benjamin pressed the button on the camera and the motor began running. First, Paul was looking around, then he looked down and as he did, Benjamin tilted the camera down and showed Paul's feet trying to fit in one of the cement footprints (James Stewart's). Benjamin tilted the camera back up so that just the top half of Paul was in the viewfinder. Then Paul began to act like he was sinking (bending his knees) while Benjamin held the camera still. Eventually Paul went below the frame and disappeared, and just in time, for the wind-up switch had completed its cycle. They thought the first scene had gone very well, and they hadn't wasted any film.

Benjamin rewound the camera and they moved down the street to the Egyptian Theater, where *Ben-Hur* was still playing. This time Paul was the camera operator, standing right in the front of the theater. First they shot Benjamin holding another title card—this one read: BENJAMIN GETS HUNGRY AND EATS THE CAMERA.

Benjamin positioned himself all the way at the end of the long forecourt, by the entrance doors to the theater. Paul signaled that the camera was running, and Benjamin began walking quickly toward it. He got closer and closer and as he did he opened his mouth as wide as he could and moved right into the lens, as if he were indeed going to eat the camera. That was a fine scene, in Benjamin and Paul's humble opinion.

Then they shot some footage of movie marquees and also the street clock at Hollywood and Wilcox (next to the Warner Cinerama Theater). After that, they went to lunch at Diamond Jim's. Paul had spaghetti and garlic bread, and Benjamin had a Shrimp Louis and garlic bread.

Next, they walked over to Bert Wheeler's House of Magic. Paul held up the next title card: THE AMAZING SWITCHEROO.

First, Paul stood in front of the magic shop, doing some wild presto-chango gestures. Then, Benjamin stopped the camera, Paul came over and stood in the exact same place with the camera while Benjamin went and stood in the exact same place where Paul had been. Paul started the camera and Benjamin did his own presto-chango gesture, as if Paul had just disappeared and he'd replaced him.

Finally, they went to C.C. Brown's and split a hot fudge sundae (Benjamin hadn't been there since he'd gone with Susan—could it really have been three years ago?). First, Benjamin shot Paul eating it, then Paul shot Benjamin eating it—on film it would look like they both had their own sundaes, or at least that was the hope.

On the bus ride home, Benjamin used the last of the film shooting through the window of the bus—capturing images of interesting sights, like Kiddieland, Lawry's Prime Rib restaurant, the miniature golf course and Marty's Bike and Candy Shop.

When Ernie got home that night, Benjamin gave the film to him. Ernie said he'd get it developed, which would take about a week.

* * *

A week later, Benjamin was presented with three rolls of 16mm film. Paul came over that night and the two of them set up the projector in Benjamin's room to view their handiwork. After several aborted tries they managed to thread the projector correctly. They aimed it at the wall and turned it on. It clattered to life noisily and after some black, suddenly, there on Benjamin's wall, the first title card appeared—KRITZER AND DALEY'S HOLLYWOOD ADVENTURES, followed by THAT SINKING FEELING. And there was Grauman's Chinese with Paul standing looking around. The color was really eye-popping and everything looked crystal clear. The sinking-in-cement bit worked well, and they laughed like idiots as if it were the funniest bit ever conceived. Benjamin did not like the way he looked in the scene where he came toward the camera as if he were going to eat it. He made a mental note never to get too close to a camera. But the idea was still funny, and they laughed at that, too.

THE AMAZING SWITCHEROO worked brilliantly. It really appeared as if Paul had vanished and been instantly replaced by Benjamin. After they finished running all the rolls of film, they ran them over again, and again after that. That night, after Paul had left, Benjamin held a screening in the den for Minnie and Ernie. Ernie laughed several times, but Minnie just sat there with her arms folded and a sour look on her face. After it was over, Ernie told Benjamin he'd done a good job—Minnie told him it was "from hunger". What other kind of comment could you expect from a Martian mother who was going through her "change of life"?

199

Benjamin placed the rolls of film safely in a box next to his Kritzerland notebook. He decided that *Kritzer and Daley's Hollywood Adventures* would be the permanent attraction at the Kritzerland movie theater.

CHAPTER SIX

Psycho, The Webcor Tape Recorder, and 8ᵗʰ Grade

August 10ᵗʰ could not arrive soon enough. That was the day *Psycho* was opening and Benjamin couldn't wait. He'd seen the coming attractions for it—Alfred Hitchcock taking a tour of the Bates Motel, and the trailer had ended with him pulling the shower curtain aside and Janet Leigh screaming. Well, Benjamin knew what was going to happen behind that shower curtain because he'd read the book, and he couldn't imagine how they'd show that scene.

Then he'd seen the big ad in the *Herald-Express* which said you had to see *Psycho* from the beginning—no one would be admitted after the movie started. It was opening in quite a few theaters, and Benjamin chose the El Rey on Wilshire. The first show was at noon and he planned to be there at eleven to be first in line. He'd called Paul to tell him the plan, but as luck would have it, Paul had a dentist appointment at noon. Paul told Benjamin he'd have to see it without him, and Benjamin assured Paul that he'd be seeing it a second time, right away no doubt, and that they'd see that showing together.

The morning of August 10th, Benjamin got up early, ate breakfast and then headed over to Leo's Delicatessen. He bought a Dad's Root Beer, had a pickle from the pickle barrel, and told Leo he was going to see *Psycho*. Leo thought *Psycho* sounded too scary, so he had no plans to see it.

Benjamin headed over to La Cienega to catch the eastbound bus on Pico. It arrived ten minutes later and he took it to La Brea, then transferred and took the northbound La Brea bus up to Wilshire. It was ten o'clock, so Benjamin took a walk and checked out the coming attraction posters at the Ritz and the Four Star movie theaters. Then he headed west to the El Rey. He looked in all the shop windows (the Miracle Mile on Wilshire had the best shops), passed the Vic Tanny Gym, passed Van de Kamp's and the Ontra Cafeteria, passed a luggage shop and several clothing shops, and finally arrived at the El Rey precisely at eleven.

Naturally, he was first in line. Within a half-hour, however, the line stretched around the block. The box-office opened, Benjamin got his ticket and hurried inside to get his tenth-row aisle seat. The theater filled quickly and was totally sold out. Benjamin could feel the anticipation in the audience, which was chattering away loudly, and his very own leg was going up and down with nervous energy.

Finally, the lights dimmed and the curtains began to part. A strange black-and-white Paramount logo came on the screen—it had weird lines through it and looked quite odd, Benjamin thought. He also thought it quite odd that they weren't showing coming attractions or cartoons. Then, suddenly, the music started, and it immediately put everyone in the audience, including Benjamin, in a state of anxiety, because the music was agitated and fierce and driving and, above all, scary. The titles were all jagged and seemed as agitated and fierce as the music which, Benjamin noted, was by his favorite, Bernard Herrmann.

The movie began slowly and Benjamin was completely caught up in it. By the time Janet Leigh had stolen the money, got a new car and pulled off the road in the pouring rain to stop at the Bates Motel, the entire audience was totally engrossed. Of course, Benjamin was ahead of them because he knew what was coming, and yet he still felt the same sense of dread as the rest of the audience (even though they didn't know what was coming, how could they not feel dread with a movie that was called *Psycho*— especially with Bernard Herrmann's music continually making everyone wholly ill-at-ease).

Then came the meeting with Norman Bates, who was played by Anthony Perkins, an actor Benjamin liked very much ever since he'd seen him in *Friendly Persuasion*. There were several moments of nervous laughter from the audience, because Norman Bates was so *peculiar*—there was just something about the way he talked and stared, especially with all those weird stuffed birds he had in the parlor. Then Janet Leigh went off to her motel room and Norman Bates peered at her through a keyhole as she undressed. Then he went back to the big house behind the motel.

She went into the bathroom, having decided to return the stolen money, and she turned on the shower. Benjamin wondered if they were going to change the scene, for surely they couldn't kill the star of the movie, Janet Leigh, and surely they wouldn't show her head being cut off like in the book. The audience began to shift uncomfortably in their seats—you could actually hear the sound of it throughout the theater. Janet Leigh then stepped into the tub shower. She closed her eyes and let the water run over her, and it seemed to make her feel better.

Then, through the shower curtain, you could see the door to the bathroom open slowly (the audience could see it, not Janet Leigh) and you could see someone, a shadowy figure, step into the bathroom. The shadowy figure moved closer to the shower curtain. Now both Benjamin's legs were both going up and down like crazy. There was a slight pause and then suddenly the shower curtain was ripped aside and there was an old lady holding a huge butcher knife—in unison, the audience screamed, as did Benjamin, and then the old woman began stabbing poor Janet Leigh, stabbing her over and over and over, with the music literally shrieking as the knife swooped down repeatedly.

The scene seemed to go on forever—Benjamin closed his eyes several times, but each time he opened them, the knife was stabbing, stabbing—Benjamin (and the rest of the audience) couldn't believe it—he could see the knife puncturing her skin and blood coming out (at least he thought he could see it—he wasn't sure what he was seeing because he kept shutting his eyes) and then the blood running down the drain. Then, just as swiftly as the murder had begun, it was over, and the old woman was leaving the bathroom as Janet Leigh grabbed at the shower curtain, then fell back and over, with her staring lifeless eye filling the screen. Then the screen was filled with the drain and the blood swirling down it.

The entire audience was in total shock—they sat there, silent (as Minnie would say, you could hear a pin drop)—no one believing what they'd just seen. Then Norman Bates cleaned up the mess that his mother had made with the knife, and watching him mop up the blood out of the tub was somehow, to Benjamin, worse than the murder itself. When Norman wrapped Janet Leigh up in the shower curtain, Benjamin was quite certain he could see Janet Leigh's breast, but luckily Minnie wasn't there to drag him out of the theater.

For the rest of the movie, there was such a palpable sense of fear in the audience that you could have cut it with the crazy mother's butcher knife. When the second murder happened, everyone screamed again, this time louder, as a poor detective got stabbed in the face—*in the face*—by the crazy mother, and as he tumbled down the stairs (Benjamin knew all about tumbling down stairs), the mother jumped on him and stabbed him repeatedly, as the music shrieked away.

At the end of the film, the sister of the murdered woman was in the cellar and saw the crazy mother sitting in a rocking chair. As she approached, Benjamin was practically climbing on his chair—looking down at his lap, then up at the screen, then down at his lap, then up at the screen, as the sister got closer to the rocking chair. And when that rocking chair had turned around and Benjamin saw the rotting corpse of mother, he literally leapt out of his chair and screamed once again along with the rest of the audience. By that time, Benjamin had totally forgotten the twist from the book and he was totally taken by surprise once again when everything was revealed.

After the movie, as the audience left the theater, they were giggling and chattering excitedly, as if they'd just come off a roller coaster ride. Benjamin just sat in his seat, unable to move. The book had been good, but the movie had been something else—it had scared Benjamin in a way he'd never been scared before. It wasn't like a monster movie, when he used to run up the aisle in fright from seeing some horrid-looking creature—no, this was much worse because it seemed so real. Still, he knew it was just a movie, and he finally got up and exited the theater. There was no way he was staying to see it again.

He walked out into the bright August sunlight and was happy to be back in a seemingly sane world. He didn't want to take the bus home, so he walked down to Fairfax, stopped at the May Company and looked around, walked down to Pico, stopped at all his usual haunts, and then finally went home.

Paul came over in the afternoon and Benjamin told him all about *Psycho* and how frightening it had been. Paul couldn't wait to see it, but Benjamin said he didn't want to go again, it was just too scary, so Paul said he'd go with his mother, who loved to be scared.

That night, Benjamin would not shower with the light on. He didn't want to see the shower tiles or the drain. And from then on, whenever he showered he always did so with the light off.

* * *

In late August, Benjamin was told that he had to begin preparations for his impending Bar Mitzvah. He remembered how hard it had been for Jeffrey to learn that whole long haftorah and Benjamin was not looking forward to it one bit. Rabbi Pressman suggested to Minnie and Ernie that the easiest way for Benjamin to learn it was if they had a tape recorder. That way, Rabbi Pressman would make a recording of the haftorah and Benjamin would be able to learn it easily through repeated listenings. That seemed like a good plan to Ernie, the only problem being that they didn't own a tape recorder. However, Ernie thought it would be fun to have a tape recorder (he was also having a very good year, business-wise), so he took Benjamin to White Front, where they chose a nice Webcor Tape Recorder.

Rabbi Pressman made the recording of the haftorah, and Benjamin began to listen to it for an hour every day. He'd read along, and then start doing the sing-songy recitation with Rabbi Pressman's voice. Within a couple of weeks he was starting to know it by heart.

When he wasn't practicing his haftorah, he and Paul were singing songs into the microphone of the tape recorder. They'd play the record of *Together, Wherever We Go* and bellow along with it, and then they'd play it back—they thought they sounded quite good, if they did say so themselves. They also did their rendition of *It's Now or Never*, singing along with Elvis, as well as *Alley-Oop*. Unfortunately, they could never get through that song without breaking up, laughing hysterically until tears were rolling down their eyes and they couldn't breathe. The reason for this was because Benjamin had spelled *Alley-Oop* backwards, suggesting to Paul that they sing it that way—

Yella-poo. From then on, all they had to do was hear the opening of the song and they'd simply dissolve into helpless heaps of insane howling laughter.

* * *

The new semester started, and Benjamin and Paul entered the 8th grade. It was, of course, not much different than the 7th grade, except for different teachers, different classes and more homework.

Every day after school, Paul would go over Benjamin's house and they'd do their homework together for an hour or so, then play records or watch *American Bandstand* or record more songs. Other days, Benjamin would hang out with Mr. Williamson, who would play him the latest records he'd gotten. Even though Paul had enjoyed tagging along to those music listening sessions, he didn't seem to have much interest in it now and he went off and did other things.

The new season of *The Twilight Zone* began, and Benjamin and Paul resumed their Friday night ritual— sitting on the beds in Benjamin's bedroom and eating their spaghetti and meatballs and watching the latest creepy episode. They both especially loved the new theme and whenever anything weird would happen at school, they'd hum it over and over again.

Benjamin's hatred of Gym class continued unabated. In fact, the only upside to it was watching the girls in their shorts play basketball or volleyball. Benjamin liked that very much. Some of the girls had started to grow breasts; Benjamin could tell, because their gym blouses had begun to stick out in that area. Oh, it wasn't like Brigitte Bardot or

Janet Leigh, but they were definitely there and Benjamin liked that very much, too. Glenda Allen looked especially good in her gym shorts and blouse, and Benjamin would always smile at her, and Glenda would always look at him and then turn away in a huff.

There was another girl that Benjamin thought was cute, too. She had long brunette hair and lanky long legs and was quite tall for a girl. She looked wonderful when playing basketball, very lithe and graceful. Her only unfortunate drawback was two huge front buck teeth that protruded from her mouth. A couple of idiot boys had nicknamed her Bucky, but her real name, Benjamin found out, was Betty Bremers. Unlike Glenda Allen, whenever Betty Bremers would see Benjamin smiling at her, she'd smile right back.

Dr. Rogers, the principal, still came on the loudspeaker every morning and this semester she was even stranger than she usually was. "Good morning students," she'd say, and then follow it with something like, "Today is Tuesday. It has come to my attention that certain students are loitering about the school grounds. We will have no loitering about the school grounds. If you are caught loitering about the school grounds you will be sent to the Vice Principal's office and you will have punishment meted out to you. Make no mistake—we will not tolerate loitering about the school grounds and punishment will be meted out. Good day."

On weekends, Benjamin and Paul would go to the movies, sometimes seeing four or five during one day and evening. They'd recently seen a double bill of *Ocean's 11* and *The Crowded Sky* (the latter was just like *The High and the Mighty*, and Benjamin was happy he hadn't seen it before he'd taken the airplane to St. Louis), *Elmer Gantry, Inherit the*

Wind (all at the Stadium), *The Apartment*, *Solomon and Sheba*, *Song Without End*, *High Time* (which was just as funny the second time around), and an amazing reserved-seats-only movie called *Spartacus*, which Benjamin liked even more than *Ben-Hur*. One Sunday, they'd gone to the Beverly to see a movie called *The Subterraneans*, and it had turned out to be about beatniks. Everyone in the movie talked like Paul's sister, Fran—it was, man this or man that, and Benjamin and Paul had laughed themselves silly over it, much to the annoyance of the other patrons. On the odd occasion when they weren't going to the movies, they'd just sit around and play records or tape record themselves being dopey, although, as the weeks went by, Paul didn't seem to be having as good a time—occasionally the fun seemed somehow forced.

As October began, Paul appeared to be preoccupied with other things—he suddenly wasn't coming over every day after school, and he even missed one of their *Twilight Zone* nights. Benjamin began to sense that something was not quite right. When he asked Paul about it, Paul assured him that everything was fine and that he'd just had other things on his mind.

CHAPTER SEVEN

Scary October

He'd been daydreaming. Off in his own little Benjamin world—thinking of that man putting his hand on Brigitte Bardot's breast in *Come Dance With Me*, thinking of Janet Leigh's breast in *Psycho*, thinking of all the girls at Louis Pasteur who were suddenly growing breasts—when without any warning at all, his new gym teacher, Mr. Shimura, was yelling in his ear and Benjamin almost fell over from the surprise of it.

"What are you doing? We are doing pushups here, Mr. Kritzer—do you see we are doing pushups here? There are boys on the ground doing pushups and you, Mr. Kritzer, are standing up staring into space like an idiot," Mr. Shimura said in an accent so thick that Benjamin had a difficult time understanding what he'd said. However, from Mr. Shimura's tone of voice, Benjamin definitely got the drift and he dropped to the ground and started to do pushups with the rest of the boys. Mr. Shimura watched him do his feeble attempts at pushups. "You are pathetic, Mr. Kritzer. I don't know what it is you're doing but it is not a pushup. Go run a lap and then get back here and do twenty proper pushups or tomorrow you will run four laps and do forty proper pushups."

Benjamin ran his lap slowly—anything was better than doing pushups, proper or otherwise. And, of course, when he was running a lap he got to watch the girls play volleyball in their shorts. As he passed them, he waved at Glenda Allen, who turned her back on him, and he smiled at Betty Bremers who smiled back at him, her two front teeth sticking out boldly and, Benjamin thought, adorably, no matter what the idiot boys said. By the time he finished his lap, Mr. Shimura was yelling at the other boys who were messing up some football formation or other. Benjamin got down and did four proper pushups (all he could manage), then ran over to where everyone was practicing. He breathed heavily, as if he'd just finished doing his twenty proper pushups. Mr. Shimura turned to him and said, "Did you do your twenty pushups, Mr. Kritzer?"

"Yes, I did," Benjamin wheezed. Butch Polsky, who was once again in Benjamin's Gym class, chimed in, "No, he didn't, he only did four. I saw him." Mr. Shimura wheeled around to Butch. "You saw him? Then you weren't paying attention to the football formation, were you, Mr. Polsky? Your business is not to watch Mr. Kritzer, your business is to keep your mind on what we're doing here. Forty pushups, Mr. Polsky. Now."

Butch, red-faced, sneered at Mr. Shimura then at Benjamin, as he got down on the ground and began doing his forty proper pushups. Mr. Shimura turned back to Benjamin. "You make me sick—go do another lap," he said, and Benjamin happily obliged.

* * *

Benjamin went to the Stadium (alone—Paul was busy) and saw a movie called *Bells are Ringing*, which he absolutely adored. It was a musical and it had the most wonderful songs—he especially loved the one Judy Holliday sang at the beginning, *It's a Perfect Relationship*, and like so many songs, he couldn't get it out of his head, so on the way home he stopped at Index Records and Radio and bought the soundtrack album. He also loved the song *The Party's Over*—it was so beautiful that he played it over and over and over.

* * *

Two weeks before Halloween, Channel Nine's *Million Dollar Movie* (*Million Dollar Movie* showed the same movie every night for a week) ran *The Beast with Five Fingers*, starring Peter Lorre.

Paul came over on Monday night, and he and Benjamin watched it together. It was a strange film about a disembodied hand which had a life of its own, crawling here and there and wherever it felt like. Benjamin and Paul loved Peter Lorre, especially his weird way of talking. At the end of the film, the disembodied hand crawled up Peter Lorre and tried to choke the very life out of him, while he kept saying, "The hand, the hand." That became their new favorite line, and wherever they went, be it the store, classes, the cafeteria, they said it whenever they could while their own hands would crawl up to their throats. "The hand, the hand," they'd say, doing Peter Lorre's voice, and then go about their business.

They watched the movie every night except Thursday, when Paul had to be home because company was coming over. That night, at nine, the phone rang and a minute later Minnie yelled that it was for Benjamin. He padded to the kitchen and picked up the receiver. On the other end of the line was silence for a moment, and then he heard Paul saying, "The hand, the hand," and then bellowing laughter and a click as Paul hung up the phone.

*   *   *

On Halloween night, Benjamin and Paul went trick or treating; Benjamin dressed as Norman Bates' mother, complete with bloody butcher knife, and Paul dressed as The Wolf Man, with fake hair all over his face. Everywhere they went, after they were given their candy, they said in their best Peter Lorre voice, "The hand, the hand."

*   *   *

November arrived and Benjamin heard the rather shocking news that the Stadium Theater had been sold and was going to become a Jewish temple. It would close its doors forever the following May. The Stadium had always been Benjamin's favorite out of the three neighborhood movie theaters. They had a big Cinemascope screen, they had stereophonic sound, and beautiful curtains; the thought that he would never be able to see a movie there again after

May filled him with ineffable sadness. It was like a part of his world was being taken away, and he'd already had the Adohr Bottling Plant taken away (the new A&P was almost ready to open), not to mention that the Orange Julius stand at Robertson and Pico had recently closed. Benjamin wondered what could possibly be taken away next.

*   *   *

The voice took Benjamin by surprise. "Why are you always smiling?"

He turned around to see who it was and standing behind him was Betty Bremers, smiling herself, her two buck teeth catching the November sunlight. "Every time I see you running on the track, you're always smiling."

"Well, I'm happy to not be doing pushups," Benjamin said, smiling.

"But you're smiling at *me*. How come?"

"I don't know. You look nice. You seem nice."

"I *am* nice."

"Well, there you are then. I'm smiling at you because you're nice."

"I smile back, have you noticed?"

Of course, if truth be told, it was hard *not* to notice, what with those two big teeth sticking out of her smiling mouth. "I have noticed. You have a nice smile."

"I have big ugly buck teeth but I'm getting braces in three months."

"You still have a nice smile," Benjamin said, and he meant it.

"Thank you, that's very nice of you to say. I hear some of the boys sometimes, when they call me 'Bucky'," she said, her smile fading a bit.

"Oh, you can't pay any attention to those idiots. They're *not* nice, they're jerks," Benjamin said, and he meant it.

"I better get to class. I just wanted to say hi. I'm Betty."

"I'm Benjamin."

"Well, see you around, Benjamin." She grinned at him again, and walked off toward the bungalows.

Benjamin and Betty ran into each other several times as the days went by—at recess, at lunch, between classes, and they always had pleasant conversations. During one of them, she asked, "Want to go to a movie sometime?" That sounded like a fine idea to Benjamin and he told her they'd have to make plans to do so very soon.

* * *

One day, after Benjamin had been visiting with Mr. Williamson after school (Mr. Williamson had introduced him to a composer named Sibelius), he'd come out of the classroom and headed toward the Airdrome gate. As he approached the gate, he happened to glance across the schoolyard and he saw five or six boys standing there, laughing raucously. He was about to turn back and leave when one of the boys moved and Benjamin saw Paul standing amongst them, and he was laughing raucously, too. He'd never seen Paul with other people; they'd always been like two loners, two peas in a pod (as Minnie would say), so it was slightly disturbing to Benjamin seeing Paul there, laughing raucously with boys Benjamin didn't know and from the looks of them probably wouldn't like.

He watched them go off (a teacher was heading in their direction—perhaps this was what Dr. Rogers meant by "loitering about the school grounds"), and then he turned and walked through the gate. All the way home he thought about what he'd seen. Maybe this was why Paul had seemed so preoccupied lately; maybe this was why he'd stopped coming over every day. But why wouldn't he tell Benjamin that he'd made some new friends? It was all very strange and Benjamin didn't know what to make of it. He also didn't know whether he should ask about it or just wait until Paul mentioned it to him. He decided on the latter because, frankly, he wouldn't even know how to bring it up.

CHAPTER EIGHT

Chilly November

With less than a month until his Bar Mitzvah, Minnie decided it was high time to get Benjamin a new Bar Mitzvah suit, new Bar Mitzvah shoes, and new Bar Mitzvah socks and underpants (like anyone was going to see his socks and underpants). Benjamin hated dressing up, hated suits and ties and hard shoes, but he knew that there was no dissuading Minnie from her quest, so off they went, their first stop: May Company.

They went to the boys' department and Benjamin tried on several suits, all of which itched him like crazy. They settled on the least itchy—it was a black and fairly non-descript two-piece suit. The salesperson took Benjamin's measurements—waist, inseam and cuff, so they could tailor the suit just for him. The salesperson kept sticking pins in the material as he'd measure and Benjamin rather liked the look of the suit with all those silver pins—he thought it would be fun to wear the suit to his Bar Mitzvah just like that. Minnie put the suit on her account, and they went off to the second stop: Karl's Shoes in Beverly Hills.

Benjamin liked Karl's because they had a weird machine where you could look through a viewfinder down at your feet. He didn't know what the machine did nor could he ever see his feet through the viewfinder, but he liked it nonetheless. He tried on several pairs of black shoes, all of which were uncomfortable. They settled on the least uncomfortable and the salesman boxed them up and Minnie paid for them.

Then they went down the street to Rudnick's and she bought him a new belt and a tie, a red tie, as well as socks and underpants. He now had his complete Bar Mitzvah wardrobe, and that included the brand new talles and yarmulke Minnie and Ernie had presented him with, which came housed in a soft blue velvet pouch.

Benjamin listened to Rabbi Pressman on the tape every day, and he'd pretty much memorized the whole haftorah. He had also begun writing his Bar Mitzvah speech. Every Bar Mitzvah boy had to give a speech in which he thanked his parents and family, his temple and his rabbi, and then talk about his hopes and goals for the future.

* * *

The Paul situation seemed to be getting worse. On certain mornings, he'd tell Benjamin that he had things to do and that Benjamin should just walk to school by himself. Benjamin would call Paul to go to a movie, but there would be an excuse. He'd call Paul to go to Leo's, but there would be an excuse. He'd offer to go to Paul's house to watch television, but there would be an excuse. They still met for lunch in the cafeteria, and they still occasionally did homework after school, but after seeing each other practically every minute of every day for the last ten months, it seemed that Paul's behavior toward Benjamin was changing radically and Benjamin didn't have a clue as to why.

When they were walking home one day, Benjamin told Paul that he was going to take Betty Bremers to the movies. Paul looked at him like he was retarded, and said, "You mean Bucky?"

"Betty. Don't call her Bucky," Benjamin said.

"Why?" Paul asked. "That's what everyone calls her."

"Since when are you 'everyone'? She's a nice girl."

"So what?"

Benjamin just looked at Paul. Certainly he and Paul had made fun of the foorps and oafs at school, but this was different. He was acting like the idiots they made fun of—the coarse, stupid, insensitive people they hated.

* * *

Benjamin and Paul did manage to catch a couple of movies—*The Magnificent Seven* (which they both loved), and a double bill at the Lido of two foreign movies—an English comedy, *Man in a Cocked Hat* and a French comedy, *The Big Chief*. Benjamin liked those a lot—he especially liked Terry-Thomas in *Man in a Cocked Hat*, because he had the largest gap between his two front teeth that Benjamin had ever seen (worse than Jeffrey's, which was pretty bad). And he thought Fernandel, who was the star of *The Big Chief*, was really funny.

They also continued their *Twilight Zone* Friday nights, and had recently seen their all-time favorite episode so far, *Eye of the Beholder*, about a woman who was wrapped in bandages because she'd just had an operation on her face—she looked different than everyone else, very ugly and hideous, and the doctors were trying to make her look normal. When the doctors had finally unwrapped the bandages, Benjamin and Paul were prepared to see some really grotesque woman because all the doctors and nurses were covering their eyes and saying, "No change, no change." Only she wasn't grotesque at all, she was a beautiful blonde lady. It was everyone else that looked grotesque. The doctors and nurses were all weird-looking, with big distorted lips and eyes and it was all too creepy and Benjamin and Paul just looked at each other with their "we're in *The Twilight Zone*" look. The next day, everywhere they went, they looked at people and said, "No change, no change." It was almost like old times.

* * *

Every day the Kritzer mailbox was filled with RSVPs for Benjamin's Bar Mitzvah. It was going to be quite a crowd, according to Minnie. She was busy making the seating arrangements for the reception, which was going to be held at the Erro, in the new banquet room that had just been added on to the restaurant. The only people Benjamin had really invited himself were Paul and, more recently, Betty Bremers, so the rest of the people were either relatives or friends of Minnie and Ernie.

Benjamin had finished writing his speech, which he was now practicing daily in front of a mirror. He had it written out very neatly, although he knew a lot of it by heart already. He had his haftorah down pat and even Rabbi Pressman was impressed with how well he recited it in their practice sessions.

* * *

He saw Paul hanging out with those same boys several other times. Days went by without them speaking and it was really beginning to bother Benjamin a lot. It was suddenly like there were two Pauls—the one he knew and had spent so much time with, the one he counted as his best and only friend—and the one who was aloof and busy and non-committal. As Thanksgiving approached, he decided he had to know what was really going on; after all, enough was enough. He spent two days trying to work up the nerve to broach the subject.

* * *

They were walking home from school, the two friends, not saying anything, not laughing like usual, not having fun like usual. When they reached Paul's house, Paul said, "See you tomorrow." Benjamin asked if he could come in for a minute, and Paul said, "I've got a bunch of stuff to do," then turned to go inside. "What's going on?" Benjamin asked. "You're always busy, you're acting all weird, you're hanging out with other people. I don't get it. Just tell me what's going on."

Paul turned around slowly and exhaled a long sigh.

"Listen, Benjamin, these guys want me to join their club—it's the Falcons, and I really want to do it."

"So? Do it. Who's stopping you?"

"They don't like that I hang around with you."

"They don't like that you hang around with me? They don't even know me."

"They don't want me to be friends with you."

"Why would *you* want to be friends with people like that? Why would you want to be in their club? We always made fun of people like that."

"I just want to. I don't have to explain it to you."

Benjamin hated this. This was Benjamin's worst nightmare. Someone you thought you could trust, someone you thought was on your side, just totally behaving like someone you didn't even know. "But what about all the fun we have, all the movies, *The Twilight Zone*, Scarantino's?" Benjamin was beginning to sound whiny, and he hated that, too. Paul just looked away, saying nothing. "Listen, are we friends or not?" Benjamin finally asked.

Paul looked back at Benjamin, then he slowly walked up to him, put his hands on Benjamin's shoulders, turned him around in the opposite direction and pushed him gently but firmly away. Then he went in the house and shut the door behind him.

It was as if Benjamin had been hit by a truck. He was in shock and he couldn't even move. How had the world turned so crazy? He just stood there trying to figure out how something like this could have happened, but no answer came to him and he finally walked home.

He was feeling so many things inside—hurt, anger, annoyance, and a million other emotions. How could a friend, a real friend, do something like this? Maybe Paul hadn't been a real friend after all; maybe he'd just hung out with Benjamin because Benjamin paid all the time. But that couldn't be—they'd laughed too much, they'd shared too much and they'd done too much. Benjamin went right to his room, closed the door and sat on his bed, cross-legged, and just thought about the last ten months. The friendship had been unexpected to begin with, but he'd come to cherish it and now, suddenly, he was back to being a loner, back to being on his own. His throat burned, his head was pounding and his heart ached.

Eventually, he went to the kitchen and ate some dinner, and then went out for a walk. He walked for an hour, just thinking about everything he was feeling. He breathed in the crisp night air, which smelled of honeysuckle and jasmine, and he walked and walked—the same streets that they'd walked together for the past ten months. They'd been a team, Benjamin and Paul had, Kritzer and Daley. As he walked, he could not get the image of Paul pushing him away out of his head. It was stuck there like a needle skipping on a record.

He walked home and went back to his room, shut off the lights and just sat there, the silence and darkness enveloping him. He turned on the record player and played their anthem, *Together, Wherever We Go.*

Wherever we go, whatever we do
We're gonna go through it together

He let the song play through, took the needle off the record, removed the record from the turntable and smashed it against the table, smashed it until it broke into tiny little pieces.

CHAPTER NINE

Turning Thirteen

He should have been happy. After all, in a couple of weeks he would turn thirteen, he would have his Bar Mitzvah, he would, according to Jeffrey, get lots and lots of money, and Christmas was coming. But he wasn't happy, he was miserable. He'd already started going down 18th Street to school so he wouldn't have to walk by Paul's house anymore, and he tried to avoid seeing Paul at school whenever possible (and when he did see him, Paul always looked away, never even acknowledging him).

It was the Kritzers' turn to have Thanksgiving dinner. Normally, he liked being around the house if Minnie was having Thanksgiving—he liked to watch the food being prepared and he liked to baste the turkey with the squirt thing—but on this Thanksgiving, Benjamin was in no mood to hang around the house, so he took the bus to Westwood

225

and went to the matinee of *Midnight Lace* at the Picwood Theater. The first scene was scary, but he soon lost interest and just sat there waiting for it to end. Walking out of the theater, he couldn't even remember what he'd just seen, other than Doris Day screaming a lot.

They had lots of company for Thanksgiving, but Benjamin pretty much stayed to himself. After everyone had left, Minnie cornered him. "What is the matter with you?"

"Nothing," Benjamin said, not wanting to have a conversation.

"Don't tell me nothing."

"Nothing. Everything's fine."

"I'm your mother, you can tell me what's wrong."

"Paul doesn't want to be friends anymore. There, happy?" Benjamin replied abruptly.

"Why?"

"Because he wants to be in some club and they don't like me and they told him not to be friends with me."

"And he listens to them? What kind of a friend is that?"

"No friend at all, I guess."

"Well, good riddance to bad rubbish. Don't even waste another breath thinking about it. Feh on him."

But Benjamin couldn't help thinking about it. It was all he thought about. Oh, he tried not to, but it was always there, nagging at him.

* * *

December arrived, and Benjamin was no better. He spent every day practicing his haftorah and his Bar Mitzvah speech, trying not to dwell on what had happened. He finally made a date to go to the movies with Betty Bremers. They spoke on the phone every now and then and Benjamin thought she was a really nice girl. It wasn't the same as with Susan, but then nothing would ever be the same as with Susan. He thought about that, how he'd had to get over Susan's moving to Montreal, that he'd had to get on with his life, but this, in a way, was worse; because even though Susan had moved he knew in his heart that she missed him and thought about him. Paul had simply pushed him out of his life and done it with such ease that Benjamin didn't know if he'd ever trust anyone again.

* * *

Benjamin and Betty went to see *Where the Boys Are* at the Four Star Theater on Wilshire. He, of course, started to walk down toward his tenth-row aisle seat, but Betty stopped him and asked if they could sit in the back of the theater because she got headaches if she sat too close. He said of course they could, and they ended up sitting in the back row of the theater. He'd never sat that far back in his life, but if it made her happy (it did), it was fine by him.

The movie was lots of fun and it perked Benjamin right up. He really liked the comedy couple, Paula Prentiss and Jim Hutton, and he *really* liked the beautiful blonde lady, Yvette Mimieux, whom he'd seen and loved when she'd played Weena in *The Time Machine*. However, the most interesting thing that happened was when Betty turned to him, smiled her goofy smile and leaned over and kissed him, hard, on the lips. First there was the surprise of it, a not unpleasant surprise at that for a just-about-to-turn-thirteen-year-old boy—then there was the pressure of her buck teeth on his lip, which really hurt because their lips were pressing together so hard.

After the movie, they went to Carnation across the street for an ice cream. Minnie picked them up and drove Betty home. Betty thanked Benjamin for the movie and the ice cream, and said she'd see him at his Bar Mitzvah party.

* * *

His birthday fell on a Thursday, so his Bar Mitzvah was a mere two days off. He wasn't really doing anything for his birthday because his Bar Mitzvah was his party, so he sat, alone in his room, and thought about things. He was a teenager now—he didn't know what that meant, really, but he did know that everything seemed to be changing. In fact, his whole world was topsy-turvy. His body was changing, the neighborhood was changing, everything was shifting and swaying and nothing seemed steady and sure.

He got out all his notebooks—his Word Notebook, the Kritzerland book, his Encyclopedia of Strange Things, everything, and he looked through them. He got out his books of 45s and looked through those as well, remembering where and how he'd heard each and every song. Once again, he looked at the photos of Susan and he felt the usual pang of missing her still, three years later. He looked at the Kritzerland book, and it still seemed like a fine place, a wonderful safe place to escape to when the world went mad. Kritzerland was his, no one else's, and no one could hurt him or harm him or cause him grief.

Then he came upon the rolls of film from *Kritzer and Daley's Hollywood Adventures*. He held the small reels in his hand and looked at them, knowing that they contained the only remnants of his only real friendship. He got out the projector, threaded it up and then closed the blinds. He sat there with his hand on the switch not quite ready to turn it on. He knew he had to put this away, he had to let go, he had to move on and be his usual Benjamin self again. He'd survived worse than this—it was hard letting go of something you cared so much about, but he knew he had to. He flipped the switch and the projector rattled to life.

There, on the wall, were the images they'd laughed at so hard. Paul, looking like he was sinking in cement, Benjamin looking like he was eating the camera; but the most astonishing of all was The Old Switcheroo, in which Paul actually turned *into* Benjamin thanks to a little camera magic. It was as if they were the same person.

He shut the projector off, then rewound the film. He was about to put the reels away when he remembered something. He remembered that when he had warts, Minnie had made him eat an apple, then they'd buried the apple core in a handkerchief in the yard. He'd thought it was stupid, and yet he'd never had another wart. He began to smile, and then he went into his parents' bedroom, opened his father's dresser drawer and got out a handkerchief. He went into the backyard and found the dirt patch where his mother had buried the apple core. He carefully wrapped the rolls of film in the handkerchief and buried them. If the buried apple core had protected him from warts—maybe the buried rolls of film would protect him from friends you couldn't count on.

He went back into the house feeling much better. He took a bite out of the hanging salami on the porch, walked out the front door, once again feeling his usual unique and special self, ready to face the next chapter in the unending serial known as his life.

EPILOGUE

Today I Am a Man

He'd gotten through his entire haftorah without a glitch, and Rabbi Pressman was patting him on the shoulder and smiling at him. Everyone in the temple was smiling, too, and Benjamin breathed a sigh of relief that could probably be heard in the San Fernando Valley. He still had his speech to do, but he was over the hard part and his leg was no longer shaking like a hula dancer.

Rabbi Pressman was saying, "Congratulations, Benjamin," and shaking his hand. He then walked away and left Benjamin alone at the podium, facing the assembled guests. There they all were—Minnie, grinning at him, Ernie, actually awake and looking proud, Jeffrey, sitting there looking like he'd rather be anywhere else, Grandma and Grandpa Gelfinbaum, Aunt Lena and Uncle

Chaz and various other aunts and uncles and cousins. Benjamin took a deep breath and began.

"Today is an important day in the life of a Jewish boy, for his Bar Mitzvah is the day when he becomes a man. Even though today I am a man, I hope I grow taller because I would hate to be a man at this height. I am still a boy's height and yet today I am a man. As I begin my teenage years, I look back on my childhood days with fondness. It feels like only yesterday that I was not a teenager—of course, it *was* only yesterday that I was not a teenager, so that explains that."

As some people began to chuckle, Benjamin continued.

"I look out and see my family—my parents, Ernest and Minnie Kritzer, my brother, Jeffrey, my grandparents and all my relatives, and I think to myself, is there anyone left on the planet Mars? I have always felt my parents came from the planet Mars, but I have realized that many children think the same thing about their parents. My parents have always meant well and done the best that they know how to do, even if my mother doesn't like when my father and I play the *Warsaw Concerto*.

"I have learned so much throughout the years. For example, from my mother I have learned that you can't look a gift horse in the mouth, I have learned that the proof is in the pudding, and I have learned that the Pope is Catholic. Those are invaluable things to know as I head out on the road to adult life. My brother Jeffrey has taught me that I don't want to be like him and I thank him for that valuable lesson.

"I hope that I will be a responsible and reasonable person, that I will make good decisions, that I will always have a sense of humor, and that I won't annoy everybody too much. I know that my family doesn't always agree on everything, and I know, like all families, we occasionally fight and get angry with each other—but my parents have provided me with a home and a bed and food and bought me lots of records and nice things, and they've taken care of me, and for that I am both thankful and grateful.

"I thank Rabbi Pressman for his patience in helping me learn the haftorah, and my father for buying the Webcor Tape Recorder which made learning it so much easier. I thank everyone who has ever shown kindness to me and I hope I will be the kind of person who will show kindness to others. In closing, I have tried to think of one thing to say which will express how I am feeling on this most momentous of days. And I believe I have found the perfect words to describe how I feel about my family, my Bar Mitzvah and my life: What is it, fish? Thank you."

* * *

Everyone was hugging and congratulating Benjamin. He was worried about how his speech had gone over with Minnie and Ernie, but they said nothing other than how proud they were, what a beautiful ceremony it had been and how handsome he looked in his new black itchy suit. Even Jeffrey had thought Benjamin's speech was funny and good.

After a while, everyone got in their cars and headed off to the Erro for the big Bar Mitzvah party.

* * *

Benjamin didn't know which was worse—all the relatives hugging and pinching his cheeks or the accordion

233

player. The accordion was fine for things like *Hava Nagila* (which the accordion man had already played four times), but it was most definitely not fine for things like *A Thousand Stars* or *Are You Lonesome Tonight*.

People were giving him envelopes with money, which Benjamin dutifully handed over to Ernie. There were large round tables everywhere where the guests sat at their designated (by Minnie) places, plus there was a little space where people could dance to the tunes of the accordion man. The noise was ear-shattering—Benjamin thought you should not put so many Jewish people in one room at one time. There were large buffet tables filled with shrimp cocktail shrimps, roast beef, turkey, cole slaw, potato salad, and plenty of desserts, and everyone seemed to be having a wonderful time.

Benjamin had to dance with Minnie and various other aunts and cousins. He did not take part when everyone got up and danced the Hora. That was where he drew the line. He sat with Betty Bremers most of the time, but she made him dance, too, when the accordion player played *Where the Boys Are* (she'd requested it), which was becoming a big hit song (and, of course, it was *their* movie). There was lots of picture taking—Benjamin with Minnie and Ernie, Benjamin with Grandma and Grandpa Gelfinbaum—well, Benjamin with everyone at the party, really. There was the lighting of the candles and the cutting of the Bar Mitzvah cake, and the party lasted for quite some time and Benjamin was there until the very end.

* * *

They got home around six-thirty and Benjamin couldn't get out of his itchy Bar Mitzvah suit fast enough. He changed into jeans and a pull-over shirt and turned on the television. He flipped around the channels without paying too much attention, then turned the television off and put on the soundtrack to *High Time*. He bopped around his room in time to the bouncy music, happy that he'd somehow survived his Bar Mitzvah.

As Side One of the album was coming to an end, Benjamin heard the phone ring. It rang twice and then he heard Minnie yell, "Benjamin, get the phone, I'm in the tub." Benjamin headed toward the kitchen to answer it—as he did, he noticed Ernie in the den, sitting in his easy chair in only his pajama top, happily snoring away.

He got to the phone by the fourth ring. He picked up the receiver and said, "Hello. Benjamin Kritzer, Man." On the other end of the line he heard a giggle.

"Well, hello, Benjamin Kritzer, Man," a girl's voice said, followed by another giggle.

His heart was suddenly in his throat—that must have been why he couldn't say anything. He stood there for the longest time before he finally spoke.

"Susan?"

ACKNOWLEDGMENTS

I would like to thank Susan Gordon, Laura Miller and Adryan Russ for their painstaking and excellent editorial expertise; Harvery Schmidt for his brilliant and evocative cover painting; my daughter Jennifer for being the warm and caring person she is; my brother Joel for not braining me and thinking I was actually fair; Craig Brockman and Mark Bakalor for helping put the cover together; everyone who took the time to write me and tell me they enjoyed *Benjamin Kritzer*; Joshua Jason for helping to spread the word; Sandy Powell, Elizabeth Cole, and Bruce Bunner of 1st Books for making the publishing process as painless and rewarding as possible; all my friends who have been and continue to be supportive and loyal; and a special thanks to all my dear Hainsies/Kimlets who had to suffer through my endless meanderings about the creation of this book. I would also like to thank the beautiful Leslie Parrish and The Three Stooges, and also Paramount Pictures for VistaVision. Finally, I know it's unseemly, but since I do have this golden opportunity, I would also like to offer a big raspberry to anyone who's ever done me dirt (you know who you are).

ABOUT THE AUTHOR

Bruce Kimmel has had a long and varied career. He wrote, directed and starred in the cult movie hit, The First Nudie Musical. He performed those same duties on his second film The Creature Wasn't Nice (aka Naked Space), with Leslie Nielsen, Cindy Williams and Patrick Macnee. He also co-created the story for the hit film, The Faculty, directed by Robert Rodriguez. As an actor, Mr. Kimmel has guest-starred on most of the long-running television shows of the Seventies, including Happy Days, Laverne and Shirley, The Partridge Family, The Donny and Marie Show and many others.

Since 1993, Mr. Kimmel has been one of the leading producers of theater music on CD, having produced over one hundred and twenty-five albums. He was nominated for a Grammy for producing the revival cast album of Hello, Dolly! and his album with jazz pianist Fred Hersch, I Never Told You, was also nominated for a Grammy. He created the critically acclaimed Lost In Boston and Unsung Musicals series, has produced solo albums for Petula Clark, Helen Reddy, Liz Callaway, Laurie Beechman, Paige O'Hara, Christiane Noll, Judy Kaye, Judy Kuhn, Brent Barrett, Jason Graae, Randy Graff, Emily Skinner and Alice Ripley, and has worked with such legends as Lauren Bacall, Elaine Stritch and Dorothy Loudon. He has also produced many off-Broadway and Broadway cast albums, including the hit revival of The King and I, starring Lou Diamond Philips and Donna Murphy, The Best Little Whorehouse In Texas starring Ann-Margret and Bells Are Ringing starring Faith Prince.

He is currently at work directing a new film, and he has adapted The First Nudie Musical for the stage. Mr. Kimmel lives in California, where he was born and raised.

Printed in the United States
1036400002B